New Zealand is a place we can all be proud of. We have some of the world's most spectacular scenery, which includes lush native bush, large stands of beech forests, crystal-clear lakes and fast-flowing rivers. As a keen hunter-gatherer I spend at least half the year tramping the hillsides in search of wild game. Over the years I have picked up many hunting skills and learnt so much about our natural resources.

Even if I don't catch anything, I never feel that my time out in the wild was wasted. For me it's just being out there that counts. Many times I have seen stunning sunrises above valleys and mountains, and stags standing in the mist roaring for dominance or large boars fighting, not even knowing that I'm there. This is what I live for. To catch an animal is a bonus.

I enjoy taking my sons out for the experience, too, and showing them how to hunt, fish and dive for kai. Teaching them at a young age helps to prepare them for the future. My boys already have a grasp on how to cook wild venison properly, how to smoke trout, eels and kahawai and how to boil up wild pork.

There are plenty of hard yards involved in lifting a 70-kilo deer or pig onto my back, then carting it through some of New Zealand's roughest terrain. I don't blame people for wondering why I do it. I suppose it's the satisfaction of getting the beast out and sharing the kai with my whanau.

FOREST

TE WAO-NUI-A-TANE

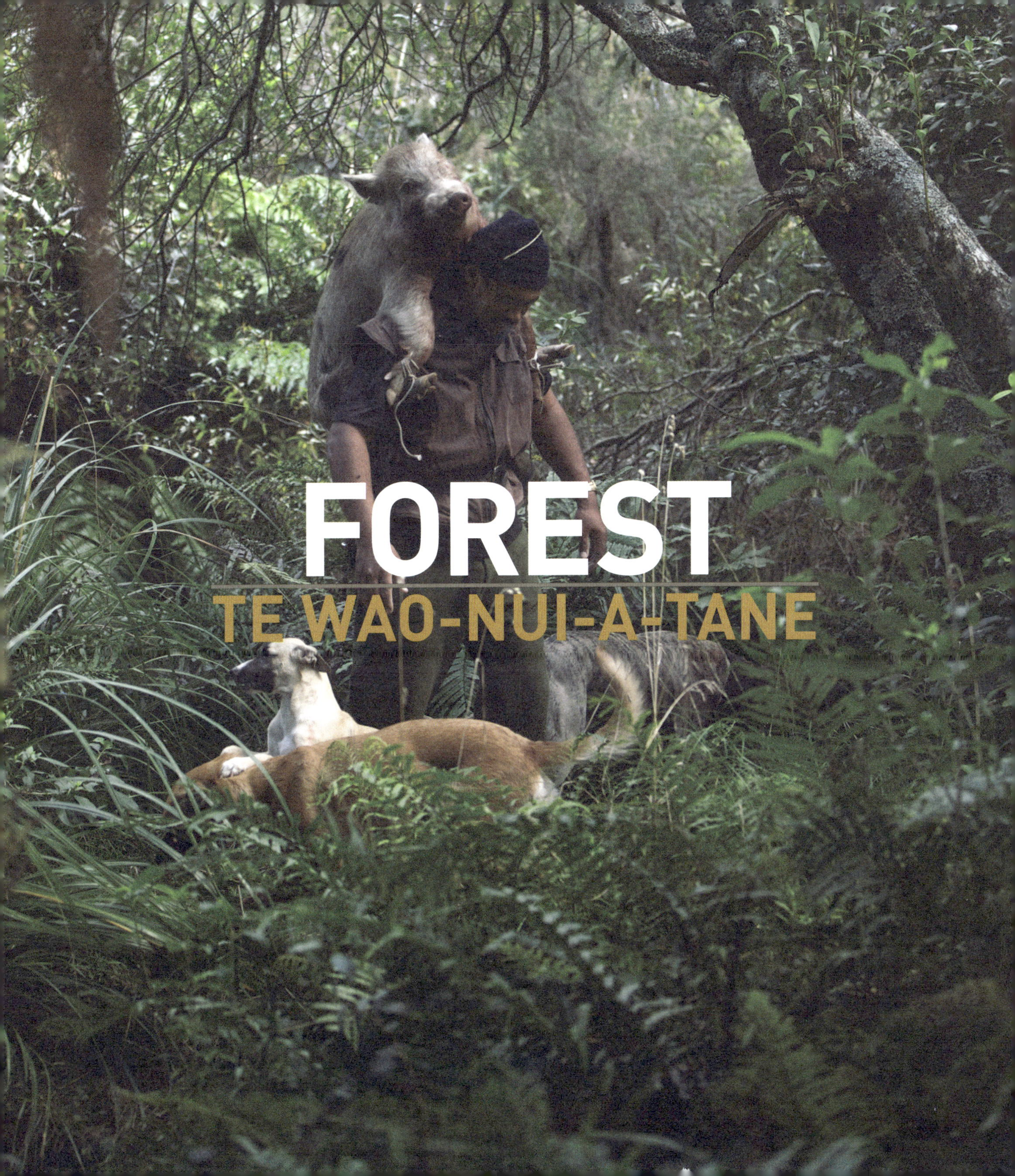

BACON HOCK & WATERCRESS SOUP
Serves 4

1 bunch watercress, plus extra
  for garnishing
2 large potatoes
1 leek, white part only
200g butter
2 litres chicken or vegetable stock
1 bacon hock
1 tablespoon thickened cream
salt and freshly ground black pepper

Wash the watercress and roughly chop. Peel and slice the potatoes, and wash and slice the leek.

In a large saucepan, melt the butter, then add the leek and potatoes. Fry gently for 5 minutes. Add the watercress and stir. Pour in the stock.

Remove any excess fat from the bacon hock. Remove meat from the bone and cut into small dice. Place the meat into the saucepan along with the bone for more flavour. Bring to the boil, then simmer for 40 minutes.

Remove the bone. Ladle the soup into a blender and liquidise. Stir in the thickened cream and season to taste. Serve hot garnished with sprigs of watercress.

PIKOPIKO & COUSCOUS SALAD
Serves 4 as a side dish

2 red capsicums
200g couscous
500ml warm water
8 pikopiko shoots
1 courgette, sliced
¼ cup basil, roughly chopped
¼ cup Italian parsley, roughly chopped
salt and freshly ground black pepper

VINAIGRETTE
200ml olive oil
80ml white wine vinegar
salt and freshly ground black pepper

Char-grill the capsicums over an open flame, then set aside to cool. Remove the burnt skin by washing under cold water. Discard core and seeds, then finely dice.

Soak the couscous in warm water for 5–10 minutes until water is absorbed and couscous is fluffy.

On a barbecue or grill plate, char the pikopiko shoots and courgette, then chop into even-sized 1cm pieces.

Mix the pikopiko, courgette, capsicums, basil, parsley, salt and pepper with the couscous.

Whisk the vinaigrette ingredients together. Season with salt and pepper and toss through the salad. Serve warm or chilled.

Pikopiko grows along the banks of creeks and streams. There are many different varieties of pikopiko, some of which are inedible. Make sure you take someone with you who knows how to identify the edible variety when looking for it in the wild.

PIKOPIKO & COUSCOUS SALAD

WATERCRESS CAESAR TORTILLA WRAPS Serves 2

4 rashers bacon, rind removed
4 slices bread, crusts removed
olive oil for drizzling
2 cups mesclun salad
handful of watercress leaves
2 tablespoons anchovies
1 tomato, diced
2 tortilla wraps
2 hard-boiled eggs, quartered

DRESSING
200ml olive oil
100ml white wine vinegar
1 egg, beaten
1 teaspoon chopped anchovies
1 teaspoon crushed garlic
1 teaspoon mustard
salt and freshly ground black pepper

Fry the bacon until crisp, then chop into small pieces.

Cut the bread into small squares and place in a baking dish. Drizzle with a little olive oil, toss well and toast in the oven at 200°C for 15 minutes. Toss during cooking process to ensure even toasting on all sides.

Blend together all the ingredients for the dressing.

In a bowl mix the mesclun, watercress, anchovies, tomato and bacon. Add a little dressing.

Divide the salad between the tortilla wraps and roll up tightly. Cut each into three and stand the sections in the centre of a plate. Sprinkle croutons around the plate and drizzle the remaining dressing on top.

Arrange the egg quarters around the tortillas.

Baby watercress is widely available and, with its bright green colour, it works well in salads and as a garnish.

Do not pick watercress when in flower because at this stage the plant is very sour. When buying watercress, check for foreign plants mixed in with the bunch and wash thoroughly to remove any dirt and insects.

PICKLED PORK, WATERCRESS, KUMARA & DOUGHBOYS Serves 4

1kg pickled pork, cut into 3cm dice
salt
2 orange (Beauregard) kumara,
  scrubbed
2 red kumara, scrubbed
6 potatoes or Maori potatoes,
  scrubbed
2 cups flour
2 tablespoons baking powder
1 bunch watercress

Place the pork in a large saucepan and cover with cold water, season with salt and bring to the boil. Cover and simmer for 2 hours, until the meat is tender.

Cut the kumara and potatoes into large chunks and add to the saucepan. Bring to the boil again and simmer for 15 minutes.

In a bowl mix the flour, baking powder, a pinch of salt and enough water to make a dough.

Roll into small balls and add to the saucepan with the watercress and simmer for a further 10 minutes. Serve hot.

Pickling the pork, especially the front shoulder and back legs, helps to tenderise the meat and stop it from drying out.

The watercress should be boiled for no more than 10 minutes to retain the nutrients and its bright green colour.

WILD PORK ROULADES WITH SWEET PRUNE & SHERRY SAUCE Serves 4

1kg pork loin
salt and freshly ground black pepper
½ cup cream cheese
¼ cup pine nuts
1 cup pitted prunes
1 bunch spinach
olive oil for frying
1 small marrow, diced
6 baby carrots, tops trimmed
50g butter

SWEET PRUNE & SHERRY SAUCE

2 nips sweet sherry
½ onion, diced
2 tablespoons pitted prunes
1 teaspoon freshly ground black pepper
100ml cream

Using a meat cleaver flatten out the pork loin and season with salt and pepper.

Mix together the cream cheese, pine nuts and prunes. Place the spinach leaves over the meat, then spread the cream cheese mixture on top.

Roll the meat up and secure with toothpicks to form a roulade. Heat a large frying pan with a little olive oil and sear all sides of the meat. Cover the pan with a lid and cook over a medium heat for 20 minutes or until the meat is cooked through. Remove from the pan and set aside.

Meanwhile, make the sauce. Using the same pan, combine the sherry, onion, prunes and pepper. Add the cream and simmer over a medium heat until slightly reduced and thickened.

In a different pan, sauté the marrow and carrots in the butter.

Cut the roulade into portions and arrange on serving plates with the sautéed vegetables. Pour the sauce over the pork and serve hot.

Using the striploin for this dish makes it easier to work with. Wild pork has its own unique flavours as a pig's diet includes berries, fern roots, huhu grubs and wild fruit.

Never hang meat during a full moon. The ultraviolet light will spoil the meat.

PHEASANT BREAST & SWEET CURRANTS ON RED CABBAGE

Serves 2

2 tablespoons olive oil

2 pheasant breasts

salt and freshly ground black pepper

pinch of paprika powder

½ cup blackcurrant jam

½ cup red- or blackcurrants

2 tablespoons sherry

½ cup beef stock

2 tablespoons clover honey

50g butter

2 cups sliced red cabbage

1 cup mashed potato

1 cup mashed kumara

fresh chives and sprig of rosemary, finely chopped

Heat the olive oil in a frying pan. Season the meat with salt, pepper and paprika and sear on both sides. Continue to cook over a medium heat for 10 minutes.

Combine the jam, currants, sherry, stock and honey and mix well. Pour this over the meat and cook until the sauce begins to caramelise (around 5 minutes), then remove meat from the pan and set aside to rest. Remove pan from heat.

Heat the butter in a clean saucepan and sauté the red cabbage until just tender. Season with salt and pepper. Reheat the mashed potato and kumara.

In the centre of each plate place some mash and red cabbage to form a cone.

Slice the pheasant breasts and arrange on top.

Drizzle the sauce over the pheasant.

Garnish with the herbs.

Pheasant is at its prime during the winter months when the birds feed up to keep warm. The fat they take on, especially around the breasts, helps to keep the meat moist during cooking.

BRAISED QUAIL ON A KUMARA & PUMPKIN RÖSTI Serves 4

3 fresh apricots, halved and stones
  removed
200ml olive oil
4 quail, boned (see below)
salt and freshly ground black pepper
½ cup fresh basil
½ cup fresh thyme
4 rashers streaky bacon
100ml red wine
½ cabbage, shredded
100g butter
100g roasted cashew nuts
2 tablespoons roasted cumin seeds

RÖSTI
2 eggs
1 cup grated kumara
1 cup grated pumpkin
salt and freshly ground black pepper

Coat the apricot halves with some of the olive oil and grill for 5 minutes. Set aside and slice when cool.

Season the quail with salt and pepper. Stuff each bird with basil, thyme and sliced apricots. Wrap with a rasher of bacon and secure with toothpicks.

Sear the birds for 5 minutes on each side in a hot pan with the remaining oil. Add the red wine, cover with a lid and simmer for 15 minutes. Remove the quail and set aside.

In a saucepan sauté the cabbage in the butter. Add the cashew nuts and cumin seeds. Season with salt and pepper.

For the rösti mix the eggs, kumara and pumpkin in a bowl and season with salt and pepper. Drop spoonfuls of the mixture into a hot oiled frying pan and brown on both sides.

To serve, place a rösti on each plate, then top each with some cabbage and a quail.

To bone out the quail, cut down both sides of the quail breast and down through the thigh bone. Follow around the back without piercing the skin. Remove the stomach frame. Leave the wing and leg bones in.

Quail are such small birds that cooking time should be kept to a minimum or they should be cooked slowly to prevent the meat from drying out. Wrapping the quail with bacon helps to keep the meat moist.

VENISON & PAUA STEAKS WITH FRESH PLUM SAUCE Serves 2

2 large paua
1 clove garlic, chopped
¼ cup soy sauce
2 tablespoons sweet chilli sauce
2 x 250g venison topside steaks
100g butter
olive oil
salt

MARINADE
2 cloves garlic, chopped
1 onion, diced
1 cup tomato sauce
4 tablespoons white wine vinegar
2 tablespoons brown sugar
1 tablespoon Worcestershire sauce
1 teaspoon mild mustard
½ fresh red chilli, chopped
salt and freshly ground black pepper

FRESH PLUM SAUCE
½ cup sugar
6 plums, halved, skin on and stones
  removed
2 tablespoons balsamic vinegar
100ml water

Tenderise the paua by placing them in a tea towel and striking the paua with a meat tenderiser. Combine the garlic, soy sauce and sweet chilli sauce in a bowl. Place the paua steaks in the marinade and refrigerate for 1 hour.

Mix together the steak marinade ingredients in a bowl. Add the venison steaks, cover and set aside.

For the sauce, combine the sugar and plums in a frying pan. Heat gently until caramelised. Keep the pan moving to avoid burning the sugar. Sprinkle in the balsamic vinegar and water. Mix well for 2 minutes while simmering, then remove from the heat.

Remove the venison and paua steaks from their marinades and place on the barbecue. Cook until the venison is medium-rare. The paua should be ready at the same time.

To serve, slice each venison steak in half lengthways. On each plate, place a venison slice topped with a paua steak, another slice of venison, then finish with paua. Top with plum sauce.

The venison and paua steaks can be cooked together for the same period of time. As soon as the steaks are rare to medium-rare, the tenderised paua steaks will also be ready.

If ageing the meat with no chiller or meat safe during the day, wrap it in mutton cloth and hang it up high in a shaded tree where there is more breeze and it's away from flies. This helps to set the meat faster, promoting tenderness and better flavour.

Another way is to place the meat in a watertight bag and place in a creek or river weighed down with rocks.

SMOKED VENISON STUFFED WITH PUHA & PIKOPIKO ON PUMPKIN, KUMARA & MAORI POTATO SMASH
Serves 4

manuka sawdust
500g venison topside, in 1 piece
1 tablespoon horopito pepper
1 tablespoon kawakawa pepper
1 tablespoon cayenne pepper
salt
150g Maori potatoes, scrubbed and
   cut into quarters
2 large kumara, scrubbed and cut into
   large dice
300g pumpkin, peeled, deseeded
   and diced
100g butter
100g puha, chopped
100g pikopiko, blanched
100ml olive oil
200ml fresh plum sauce (see page 24)

Heat a smoker containing manuka sawdust.

Season the venison with horopito, kawakawa and cayenne peppers and salt. Smoke for 10 minutes on high, then turn off and allow the meat to rest.

Meanwhile, boil the potatoes, kumara and pumpkin in a saucepan of salted water. Once cooked, drain and add the butter and a pinch of salt then, using a spoon, mix together quickly to form a coarse mash.

Make an 8cm incision three-quarters of the way through the centre of the meat and stuff with puha and pikopiko. Tie the meat with butcher's string at regular intervals to secure the stuffing. In a frying pan heat the olive oil, sear both sides of the meat and cook until medium-rare. Remove from the pan and allow to rest before slicing.

To serve, place a heaped spoonful of pumpkin, kumara and potato smash on to 4 plates, top with slices of venison and drizzle with plum sauce.

Ageing wild venison in a chiller for at least four days helps to tenderise the meat, especially the back leg muscles.

It's a must to blanch the pikopiko in boiling, salted water for at least 10 minutes to soften.

VENISON & EGGPLANT STACK Serves 2

6 x 100g venison medallions
salt and freshly ground black pepper
6 tablespoons peanut oil
100ml red wine
200ml beef stock
100g mixed berries
1 eggplant
rosemary for garnish

Season the medallions with salt and pepper. Add the oil to a hot frying pan, sear the meat to medium-rare, then remove from pan.

Add the red wine to the pan and reduce by half. Add the stock and the berries, and simmer for 10 minutes.

Cut the eggplant crosswise into slices, sprinkle with salt and leave for 5 minutes to draw out the bitterness. Pat dry. In a separate pan, fry the eggplant slices in more peanut oil.

To serve, place a venison medallion in the centre of a plate, top with a slice of eggplant, then continue alternating the medallions and eggplant until all used, finishing with a medallion. Drizzle the berry sauce over and garnish with rosemary.

Venison steaks should be cooked rare to medium-rare for maximum flavour. It is a very lean meat and can become dry if overcooked.

Never waste kai. If you shoot an animal, bring out all the meat, not just the back steaks or back legs – even if you have to make a couple of trips.

Life in the country definitely has its advantages. It's peaceful, picturesque and there's always plenty to do. These days we live next to a farm where I have spent many hours walking, biking and even jogging up and down the hills.

As kids, my brothers and I would help our local farmer during the school holidays, checking on stock and helping out with the general farm work. We loved it, often staying out most of the day on our horses. By lunchtime, of course, there were some very hungry young boys to be fed, having worked up quite an appetite.

There was one lunchtime cook-up that I will never forget. We'd been rounding up ewes for dog tucker and our rumbling stomachs meant only one thing was on our minds – mutton chops cooked on corrugated iron over an open flame for lunch. It was a little on the tough side but I still remember thinking it was the sweetest meat I had ever tasted – probably because I was so ravenous.

Soon after this I started hunting in earnest and the local farmers were always very accommodating, letting me hunt on their property. The rabbits and pheasants that roamed the local farmland became my primary targets. I started with a small air pistol which soon evolved into a .22 rifle. That took care of business!

From lamb to beef, chicken to ostrich, every meat has its own unique qualities and flavour. Throughout this section you will pick up some really useful tips for preparing and cooking farmed meats and produce. Enjoy!

FARM
TE PAAMU

CARPETBAG STEAK WITH WATERCRESS SALAD Serves 4

4 x 200g beef eye fillet medallions
8 Pacific or Bluff oysters
salt and freshly ground black pepper
4 stems rosemary, leaves chopped
4 rashers streaky bacon
olive oil for frying

WATERCRESS SALAD

1 bunch watercress
400g mesclun
4 rashers streaky bacon, fried and
  chopped
¼ rock melon, diced
1 red onion, sliced
1 tomato, diced
1 red capsicum, cored and sliced
¼ cup roasted assorted nuts
2 tablespoons grated parmesan
2 tablespoons extra virgin olive oil
salt and freshly ground black pepper

Cut 2 pockets into each beef medallion. Place an oyster inside each pocket and close up with a toothpick.

Season with salt and pepper, and rub the rosemary all over the meat.

Wrap a rasher of bacon around each medallion and secure with a toothpick.

For the salad, wash the watercress and mesclun, then tear the leaves into small pieces and place in a bowl. Sprinkle the bacon over the greens.

Toss the melon, onion, tomato, capsicum and roasted nuts through the salad.

Sprinkle the parmesan on the salad, drizzle with olive oil and finish with a little salt and plenty of pepper.

Heat some oil on a barbecue or in a frying pan. Sear the medallions on all sides, reduce the heat and cook until medium-rare for 6-7 minutes. Serve immediately with some watercress salad alongside.

Bluff oysters are a winner for the carpetbag steak, but Pacific oysters do just as well, especially when they are fat and creamy. If eye fillet is too expensive, Scotch fillet or rump will do just fine, plus you can add more oysters to the bigger cuts of meat.

ROAST SCOTCH FILLET WITH GARLIC & ROSEMARY ON TURNIP TOPS & MAORI POTATOES Serves 4

1kg Scotch fillet, in 1 piece
6 cloves garlic
2 fresh rosemary sprigs
salt
20g horopito pepper
20g kawakawa pepper
20g cayenne pepper
200ml olive oil
1 large carrot, chopped
1 large onion, chopped
200ml port
2 litres beef stock
2 bunches turnip tops, chopped
200g butter
1kg Maori potatoes, scrubbed
 and halved
freshly ground black pepper

Cut 6 x 1cm-deep slots into the scotch fillet. Push each clove of garlic into a slot along with some rosemary leaves. Season the meat with salt and the three peppers.

Heat 100ml olive oil in a cast iron saucepan over an open fire or gas hob. Sear the fillet on all sides once the oil is hot. Add the carrot and onion and stir-fry for 5 minutes. Add the port, let it bubble, then add half the beef stock. Cover with a lid and cook the meat until medium-rare (around 30 minutes).

In another saucepan, bring some water to the boil. Add salt, the turnip tops and half the butter, cover with a lid and simmer for 10 minutes until the turnip tops are soft.

Boil the potatoes in a saucepan of salted water. Once tender, drain the potatoes, slice and sauté in olive oil and the rest of the butter. Season to taste.

Once cooked, remove the fillet and set aside. Add the remaining beef stock to the pan, stirring all the time to extract the flavours from the bottom of the pan. Bring to the boil and reduce stock to a sauce consistency.

Strain the turnip tops, place the potatoes on the serving plates followed by the turnip tops. Slice the beef, arrange on the vegetables and finish with the sauce.

You can add pumpkin and kumara to the potatoes for colour and different flavours.

Always allow meat to rest once cooked to ensure it will be tender and juicy when carved. I was taught to allow 5 minutes' rest per 500 grams.

BARBECUED OSTRICH ON CHINESE GREENS WITH OSTRICH EGG Serves 2

olive oil for frying
2 shallots, finely diced
3 cloves garlic, finely chopped
2 heads Shanghai bok choy, sliced
1 stalk celery, sliced
2 spring onions, sliced
100g bean sprouts
3 large Portobello mushrooms, sliced
100g snowpea shoots
¼ cup white wine
3 tablespoons freshly chopped thyme
1 tablespoon Dijon mustard
salt and freshly ground black pepper
1 ostrich egg
4 x 120g ostrich medallions
100ml soy sauce

Heat a frying pan with a little olive oil until hot, then sauté the shallots and garlic until soft. Add the bok choy, celery, spring onions, bean sprouts, mushrooms and snowpea shoots. Add the white wine, 2 tablespoons of the thyme and the Dijon mustard. Check seasoning. Sauté for 5 minutes then set aside.

Whisk the ostrich egg in a bowl and season with salt and pepper. Heat a frying pan with a little olive oil. Pour in the egg and, using a fork, bring the edges to the centre until fully cooked like an omelette. Tip onto a chopping board and slice into thin strips, then fold into the vegetables.

Season the ostrich meat with salt and pepper, mix with the remaining thyme, dip into the soy sauce and barbecue for 5 minutes until medium-rare.

Divide the vegetables between 2 plates. Slice the meat and fan out on top of the vegetables. Serve hot.

Like venison, ostrich meat should be fried or grilled until rare to medium-rare only. The meat is lean and low in cholesterol and has the healthy heart tick of approval.

LAMB'S FRY Serves 2 as an entrée

50ml olive oil
1 onion, chopped
2 large mushrooms, chopped
2 cloves garlic, crushed
2 lamb kidneys
1 lamb heart
150g lamb liver
1 ham steak
1 tablespoon beef stock powder
100g flour
1 cup hot water
2 large vol au vents
2 spring onions, sliced for garnishing

Preheat the oven to 180°C. Heat the olive oil in a large saucepan. Fry the onion, mushrooms and garlic for 3 minutes. Chop the kidneys, heart, liver and ham into even-sized dice and add to the pan. Sauté the meat quickly.

Add the beef stock powder and flour. Stir well to combine all the ingredients.

Pour in the hot water, stirring continuously. Cook for 15 minutes until the meat is tender.

Heat the vol au vents, then fill with the lamb's fry mixture. Garnish with spring onions and serve hot.

There's a distinct flavour and texture to offal that many people enjoy. If you think the offal may be too strong for your guests, boost up the sauce with chopped roasted garlic.

VEAL FILLET WITH BITTERSWEET TOMATO MEAT GLAZE Serves 2

2 x 210g veal loin or fillet
salt and freshly ground black pepper
olive oil for frying
10 cherry tomatoes
juice and zest of 1 lemon
2 tablespoons redcurrant jam
100ml beef stock
50ml port
60g redcurrants
80g leeks, both white and green parts,
  finely diced then blanched
small handful of fresh herbs

Thinly slice the veal and season with salt and pepper.

Heat some olive oil in a hot pan and sear the meat quickly, then remove and set aside to rest. Keep warm.

To the same pan add the tomatoes and lemon zest. Cook quickly to coat with the pan juices, then remove from the pan and set aside. Add the jam, stock and port to the pan. Simmer and reduce by half, stirring continuously with a wooden spoon. Add the lemon juice, then strain the sauce into a clean saucepan. Add the redcurrants and leek, bring the sauce back to the boil and add the cooked tomatoes.

Add the veal back to the sauce to warm through then spoon onto a warm plate. Drizzle any excess sauce over the meat and top with herbs.

LAMB'S FRY

SMOKED LAMB RACK, HERBED PUMPKIN, KUMARA & NEW POTATOES WITH A PORT & GINGER SAUCE Serves 3

6 boned lamb racks
salt and freshly ground black pepper
manuka sawdust
3 tablespoons wholegrain mustard
1 cup chopped fresh herbs, plus extra
  for the vegetables
2 kumara, peeled and cut into large dice
¼ pumpkin, peeled, deseeded and cut
  into large dice
3 new potatoes, scrubbed and cut into
  large dice
1 tablespoon olive oil
1 red onion, cut into wedges
1 bulb garlic, halved crosswise
2 lamb kidneys, cut into large dice
9 cherry tomatoes

PORT & GINGER SAUCE
½ cup port
1 cup lamb stock
1 x 6cm piece fresh root ginger, chopped
3 sprigs rosemary, leaves chopped

Preheat the oven to 180°C. Trim the silver skin from the lamb and season the meat with a little salt and pepper. Line the bottom of a baking dish with aluminium foil and cover with manuka sawdust. Place a wire rack over the dish, place the lamb on the rack, then cover with aluminium foil. Place the baking dish on a hot gas hob for 10 minutes. Turn the lamb over, cover and smoke for a further 10 minutes.

Remove lamb racks, rub the mustard on to the loins, then coat with the chopped herbs. Place in another baking dish and roast in the oven for 10 minutes until medium-rare. Remove from the oven and allow to rest for 5 minutes.

Boil the kumara, pumpkin and potatoes in salted water until tender, ensuring they do not overcook. Drain and tip onto a large sheet of aluminium foil. Drizzle with olive oil and mix in some chopped herbs, the onion and garlic. Season with salt and pepper. Fold the aluminium foil into a parcel and place in the oven for 15 minutes.

Thread the kidneys alternately with the cherry tomatoes on to 3 skewers. Drizzle with a little olive oil, season then sauté in a hot pan for 5 minutes.

To make the sauce, remove the lamb from the dish and pour in the port and stock. Add the ginger and rosemary and bring to the boil. Simmer until reduced by half.

To serve, place a spoonful of vegetables in the middle of each plate, cut the lamb racks into cutlets and arrange on top of the vegetables. Place a kidney kebab on the side and finish off with the port and ginger sauce.

Lightly smoking lamb for a short period is all that is needed to flavour the meat. Manuka is the most common native tree used for smoking sawdust and is available at hunting and fishing stores throughout New Zealand.

LAMB & CABBAGE PARCELS
WITH SWEET SAUCE
Serves 2 as an entrée

2 large red cabbage leaves
2 large green cabbage leaves
2 lamb rumps, diced
salt and freshly ground black pepper
3 tablespoons olive oil
½ onion, diced
1 teaspoon crushed garlic
2 sprigs of mint leaves, chopped
1 cup cooked brown rice
4 tablespoons pine nuts
spring onion strips for tying parcels

SWEET SAUCE
100ml orange juice
50ml mint sauce
2 tablespoons honey
1 tablespoon toasted sesame seeds

Preheat the oven to 180°C.

Steam or blanch the cabbage leaves for no longer than 5 minutes.

Season the lamb with salt and pepper. Heat the olive oil in a frying pan until hot, then add the lamb pieces, onion and garlic and fry for 5 minutes.

Add the mint and cook for 5 minutes. Add the brown rice, stir, then add the pine nuts.

Remove the stems from the base of the cabbage leaves. Spoon even amounts of the lamb mixture into the centre of each cabbage leaf, fold the sides in, then roll into parcels. Tie each parcel with the spring onion strips. Arrange in a serving dish and keep hot.

For the sauce heat all the ingredients in a small saucepan for 2 minutes. Pour the sauce over the parcels and bake in the oven for 20 minutes.

CURRIED LAMB SHANKS WITH EGGPLANT Serves 4

4 lamb shanks, trimmed of excess fat

olive oil for frying and drizzling

2 cups lamb or beef stock

1 eggplant, sliced crosswise into
  2cm slices

salt and freshly ground black pepper

2 cups cooked rice

½ cup sliced cucumber

½ cup deseeded and sliced
  red capsicums

juice and zest of 1 lemon

balsamic vinegar

MARINADE

1 teaspoon minced garlic

2 level teaspoons curry powder

1 teaspoon crushed fresh root ginger

1 tablespoon hot curry paste

½ teaspoon coriander paste

½ teaspoon saffron powder

150ml natural yoghurt

2 tablespoons oil to help seal the
  lamb shanks

For the marinade, combine all the ingredients and brush over the lamb shanks. Set aside for 30 minutes to marinate.

Brown the shanks all over on a hot grill plate with a little oil, then place in a heavy-based saucepan over a high heat and ladle over a little stock to create steam. Repeat every 15 minutes, turning the shanks until cooked. This will take about 1½ hours. Set aside for 5 minutes to rest.

Meanwhile, season the eggplant and fry quickly in a little oil until cooked, then set aside.

Place a mound of rice in the centre of each plate, then arrange the eggplant around the rice. Place a shank on top of each serving, then top with the vegetables, lemon juice and zest. Drizzle the perimeter of the plate with a little balsamic vinegar and olive oil.

When buying shanks check with the butcher that they are lamb and not mutton. Lamb shanks are much softer and tastier, however mutton can also be used.

TUSCAN CHICKEN WITH
CAPSICUM CHILLI SAUCE Serves 2

¼ cup breadcrumbs
3 cloves garlic
3 tablespoons Tuscan spice
1 tablespoon parsley flakes
4 tablespoons olive oil, plus extra
  for frying
¼ cup cashew nuts
salt and freshly ground black pepper
4 chicken thighs, skinned
  and boned
olive oil for frying
1 onion, diced
1 cup dried orzo
2 cups chicken stock
1 spring onion, sliced

CAPSICUM CHILLI SAUCE
4 red capsicums
2 tablespoons olive oil
¼ tablespoon crushed fresh chillies
½ cup tomato juice
2 tablespoons chopped parsley
salt and freshly ground black pepper

Preheat the oven to 180°C. In a blender place the breadcrumbs, garlic, Tuscan spice, parsley flakes, olive oil, cashew nuts, and salt and pepper. Blend to a fine paste. Coat the chicken thighs with this mixture.

Roast the chicken in the oven for 15 minutes.

In a saucepan, heat a little olive oil. Stir in the onion and orzo and sauté for 2 minutes. Add the chicken stock and simmer until orzo is tender. Mix in the spring onions.

Meanwhile, make the sauce. Halve the capsicums, sprinkle the skin side with olive oil and roast in the oven for 5-10 minutes or until the skin is black. Cool, then remove the skins, cores and seeds. Place in a blender with the chillies, tomato juice and parsley. Blend until smooth. Season to taste.

Serve 2 chicken thighs on a bed of orzo in the centre of each plate, with the sauce around the side. Serve hot.

TAGLIATELLE WITH SUNDRIED TOMATO & CHILLI PESTO Serves 2

200g tagliatelle

100ml olive oil, plus extra for pasta

2 sundried tomatoes

1 tablespoon chilli pesto (see below)

½ cup mixed olives, pitted

1 teaspoon crushed garlic

few sprigs of fresh basil, plus extra
  for garnishing

100ml white wine

salt and freshly ground black pepper

1 large tomato

200g buffalo mozzarella

fresh basil for garnishing

extra virgin olive oil to serve

balsamic vinegar to serve

CHILLI PESTO

1 fresh red chilli

2 sundried tomatoes

2 tablespoons roasted pine nuts

6 fresh basil leaves

4 tablespoons grated parmesan

4 tablespoons olive oil

Cook the tagliatelle in plenty of boiling salted water until al dente (firm to the bite). Strain, sprinkle a little oil through to prevent the pasta sticking and set aside.

Heat the olive oil in a frying pan, then add the sundried tomatoes, pesto, olives, garlic and the basil and fry gently for 2-3 minutes. Add the white wine and season to taste. Bring to a simmer.

Lightly fold in the pasta.

Slice the tomato and mozzarella and arrange around the edge of a serving plate. Garnish with fresh basil leaves and sprinkle with extra virgin olive oil and balsamic vinegar. Place the tagliatelle in the centre of the plate and serve.

To make the chilli pesto, place all the ingredients in a food processor and blend until smooth.

STUFFED ROASTED CAPSICUMS WITH ROASTED RED CAPSICUM SAUCE

Serves 2

2 large red capsicums
100g pumpkin, peeled,
  deseeded and diced
1 teaspoon sesame seeds
2 tablespoons honey
100ml olive oil, plus extra
  for sprinkling
1 teaspoon crushed garlic
½ onion, diced
1 courgette, sliced and blanched
1 carrot, sliced and blanched
60g button mushrooms, sliced
4 beans, sliced and blanched
salt and freshly ground black pepper
50g feta cheese
1 cup cooked couscous

ROASTED RED CAPSICUM SAUCE

5 tablespoons olive oil
2 red capsicums, roasted, skinned,
  cored and chopped
1 shallot, finely chopped
6 fresh basil leaves
1 tablespoon balsamic vinegar
100ml dry white wine
2 tablespoons honey
salt and freshly ground black pepper

Preheat the oven to 180°C. Slice off the top of the capsicums, remove the cores and seeds, then place in an ovenproof dish and set aside.

Place the pumpkin in a small roasting dish, sprinkle with sesame seeds, a little honey and olive oil, then cover with aluminium foil. Bake in the oven for 20 minutes until just cooked, but still firm.

In a saucepan heat the olive oil, add the garlic and onion, and sauté until soft. Toss with the courgette, carrot, mushrooms, beans and the baked pumpkin and season to taste.

Spoon the vegetable mixture into the capsicums, top with a slice of feta and sprinkle with olive oil. Bake in the oven for 10 minutes.

Meanwhile, make the sauce. Heat the oil in a pan and sauté the capsicums and shallot for 5 minutes. Add the basil, vinegar, wine and honey. Simmer for 10 minutes, then blend sauce in a food processor. Season to taste.

Remove capsicums from the oven and serve on a bed of couscous with the sauce drizzled over the top.

Cook the vegetables for the filling just a little, so they remain firm. That way they will not end up looking like a mash or casserole when spooned into the capsicums.

VEGETARIAN FILO PARCELS
Serves 4 as an entrée

3 tablespoons olive oil
1 courgette, thinly sliced
2 carrots, sliced into matchsticks
1 stick of celery, thinly sliced
5 mushrooms, sliced
1 red onion, sliced
1 each red, yellow, green
  capsicum, sliced
½ cup bean sprouts
¼ cup snowpea shoots
¼ cup roasted mixed nuts
salt and freshly ground black pepper
150g butter, melted
12 sheets filo pastry
100g camembert cheese,
  cut into 4 wedges
½ avocado, cut into 4 wedges
fresh plum sauce (optional)
  (see page 24)

Heat the olive oil in a saucepan, add the courgette, carrot, celery, mushrooms, onion, capsicum, bean sprouts and snowpea shoots and lightly sauté.

Add the nuts and season to taste. Remove from the heat and strain. Preheat the oven to 180°C.

Using a pastry brush, brush some butter onto a sheet of filo pastry, lay a sheet on top and brush with butter, lay another sheet on top and brush with butter again.

Place a large spoonful of the vegetable mixture on one end of the pile of pastry, top with a wedge of camembert and avocado, fold the pastry over, tuck in the sides and roll to make a parcel. Brush the top with melted butter. Repeat the process to make 3 parcels. Bake in the oven for 15 minutes or until golden brown. Serve hot or cold with plum sauce.

You can make smaller vegetable parcels to serve under freshly poached snapper or tarakihi. You can also add diced rockmelon or honeydew melon to the filo parcel just before baking.

On many a dark night during my youth, Dad and friends would head out on a little boat across Lake Rotoiti to catch kewai. As a very young child, I was deemed too little to tag along on the expeditions, much to my dismay. So, needless to say, I could hardly wait until morning to check out the previous night's catch, which would be sitting in a large tub on the kitchen bench.

I remember one particular morning I jumped out of bed and headed for the kitchen. I didn't even make it down the hallway as crayfish were crawling all over the floor. They were everywhere – under the table, behind the fridge and under the oven. Well, someone forgot to cover the bin with a lid, didn't they? I found myself catching some crays that morning, without even getting wet.

Our rivers, lakes and wetlands contain plenty of sweet and succulent food. The winter mornings in duck-shooting season start with a bang. Eels migrate up and down the channels and beautiful rainbow trout rise early to catch the fattest bugs.

Before I took up hunting I was mad on fishing for those elusive trout.

I thank my koro (grandfather) for taking the time to teach me the basics. In no time at all I was hooked! Before school, after school and any other opportunity I could get, I'd take my fishing gear and head out to the water to try my luck.

On the weekends I would get to my possie at the Ohau Channel as early as 4am to ensure I scored the top spot. Fishing started at 5am for most of us, but sometimes the odd reel would unwind 10 minutes early. Okay, I couldn't help it!

Our table was always laden with baked, boiled, fried or smoked trout all year round. Trout is such a versatile fish which means that, with just the minimum of effort, trout for dinner is never boring.

Experimenting with trout is definitely the key – have you ever tried raw trout mixed with coconut cream, onions and tomatoes? Trust me, it's delicious.

There's an art to smoking trout – or any fish for that matter – but that all comes down to practice. Don't smoke fish too fast, use the right wood or sawdust for better flavour and try out different seasonings to suit your taste buds.

LAKES & RIVERS

NGA ROTO ME NGA AWA

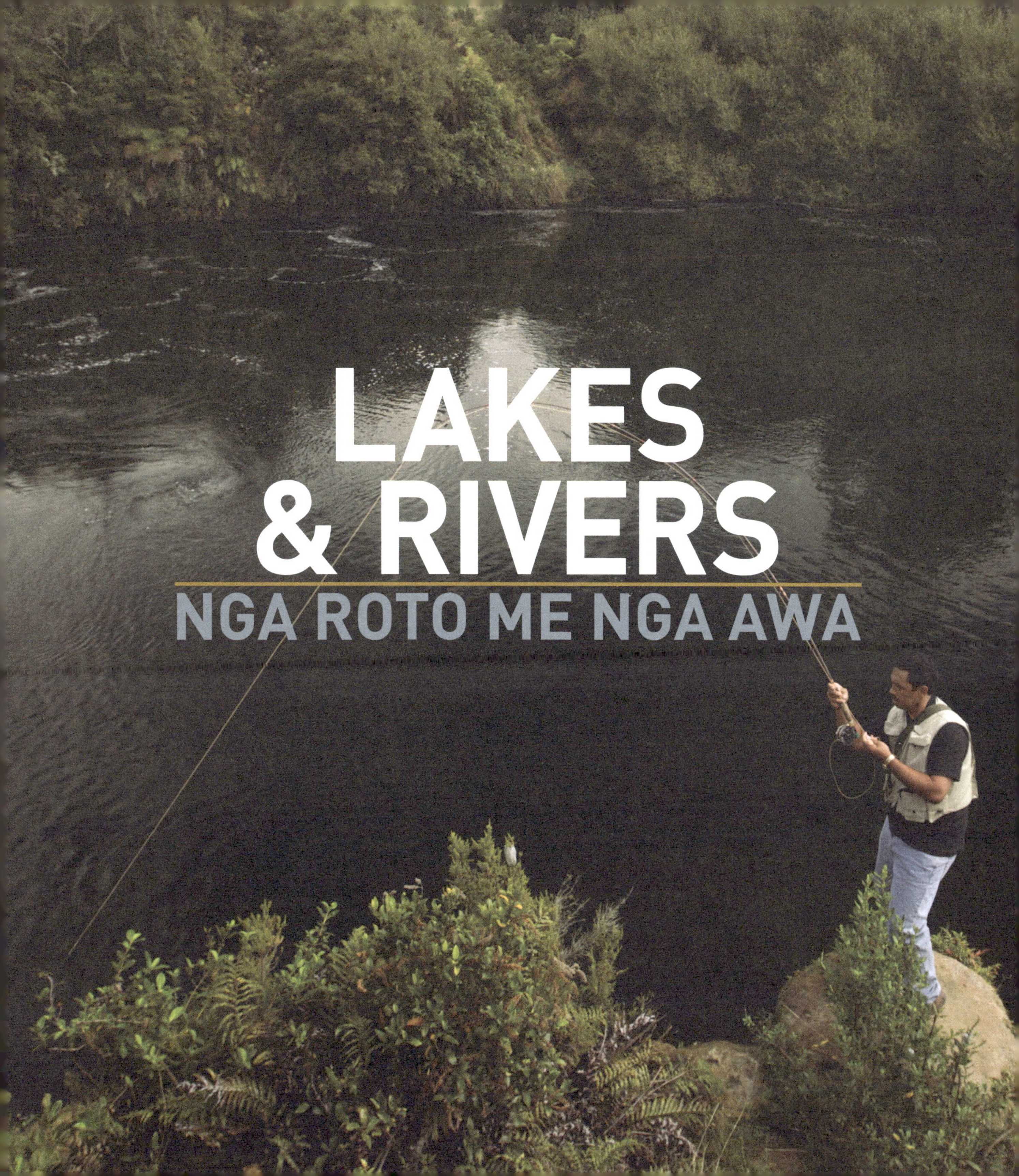

DUCK & CHICKEN LIVER PÂTÉ
Makes enough for 8

250g butter
½ onion, finely chopped
500g duck livers
500g chicken livers
1 tablespoon crushed garlic
salt and freshly ground black pepper
1 tablespoon gelatine
10 rashers bacon, rind removed

Preheat the oven to 180°C. In a saucepan, melt the butter and sweat the onion until soft, then add the livers, garlic and seasoning. Continue to fry for about 10 minutes. Remove from the heat. Slightly undercooking the livers before blending helps to ensure the pâté is pink-coloured and has a smooth texture. If overcooked, the pâté will be dry, brown and crumbly.

Dissolve the gelatine in a little water over a low heat, then add to the liver mixture.

Pour the liver mixture into a blender and process until smooth. Line a loaf tin with the bacon crossways so it hangs over the side.

Pour the liver mixture into the pan and fold the bacon over to cover. Cover with aluminium foil, then place the dish in a water bath and bake in the oven for 1 hour. Remove from the oven and allow to cool. Cut into slices using a hot knife and serve.

DUCK & VEGETABLE BROTH
Serves 6–8

1 duck prepared in any way, plucked
  and cleaned, chopped into quarters
2 litres cold water
600g vegetables (celery, carrots,
  leek and onions), diced
100g barley
1 bouquet garni
salt and freshly ground black pepper
1 tablespoon chopped parsley

Place the duck in a large saucepan, add the water, bring to the boil and skim fat from the surface. Cover and simmer for 1 hour.

Add the vegetables, barley, bouquet garni and season. Simmer for 20 minutes or until the vegetables are soft.

Take the duck from the broth. When cool enough to handle, remove the skin and discard. Pull all the meat from the bones and cut into neat dice the same size as the vegetables. Return the meat to the broth.

Bring back to the boil, skim the surface again and adjust the seasoning. Add the chopped parsley and serve.

Wild duck is ideal for this recipe. The gamey flavour boosts the broth, but extra cooking time may be needed to tenderise the meat.

ROASTED FRESHWATER PRAWNS
ON COCONUT JASMINE RICE Serves 4

COCONUT JASMINE RICE

4 cups water

1 tablespoon instant chicken
  stock powder

2 cups jasmine rice

5 tablespoons coconut cream

2 tablespoons chopped parsley

ROASTED FRESHWATER PRAWNS

20 freshwater prawns

¼ cup extra virgin olive oil

freshly ground black pepper

sea salt

¼ cup chopped fresh thyme

2 cloves garlic, chopped

6 lemon wedges for garnishing

chopped parsley for garnishing

For the rice, bring the water and chicken stock to the boil. Add the rice, reduce the heat and stir continuously for 10 minutes to prevent sticking and burning. When the rice is cooked it should be nice and fluffy. Gently fold in the coconut cream and parsley while the rice is still hot. Set aside.

For the prawns, preheat the oven to 200°C. Carefully split each prawn in half lengthways and remove the vein. Place the prawns in a baking dish flesh side up and sprinkle with the olive oil, a little pepper and sea salt, and scatter the thyme and garlic over.

Grill or roast the prawns for 4 minutes or until the flesh is firm.

Serve the prawns on the jasmine rice and garnish with lemon wedges and parsley.

For extra bite, sprinkle fresh chopped chilli on the prawns before grilling.

ITALIAN-STYLE FISH & FRESHWATER CRAYFISH SOUP Serves 4

60ml olive oil
3 large cloves garlic, chopped
½ large green capsicum, deseeded
  and finely chopped
10–12 freshwater crayfish, shells on
½ teaspoon chilli paste
400g can diced Italian tomatoes
4 small stalks fresh oregano
6 leaves fresh basil, chopped
1 teaspoon salt
freshly ground black pepper
250ml fish stock
1kg firm white fish fillets, cut into
  large pieces (use the cheapest
  fish available)
8 green-lipped mussels, debearded
  and scrubbed
½ cup chopped parsley
olive focaccia bread to serve

Heat the oil in a large wok or frying pan, add the garlic and capsicum, and fry gently until the garlic becomes golden brown. Add the crayfish and chilli paste. Toss to mix all the ingredients together.

Pour in the tomatoes. Add the oregano, basil and salt and black pepper to taste.

Pour in the stock and bring to the boil. Reduce the heat and simmer gently, covered, for 10 minutes, then add the fish, mussels and parsley. Simmer for a further 5 minutes until the fish is just cooked through and the mussels have opened. Serve hot with fresh olive focaccia bread.

If you can't source any freshwater crayfish, you can use 16–20 whole green prawns from your local seafood outlet. Add a couple of drops of Kaitaia Fire to the soup for an extra sting.

BAKED WHOLE TROUT Serves 6

1 x 2.5kg trout
1 tablespoon horopito pepper
salt
1 brown onion, halved
6 bamboo skewers, soaked in water
1 clove garlic, chopped
1 red capsicum, cored, deseeded and
  thinly sliced
1 green capsicum, cored, deseeded and
  thinly sliced
1 red onion, sliced
1 carrot, thinly sliced
2 tomatoes, diced
4 basil leaves, chopped
freshly ground black pepper
3 tablespoons butter
100ml olive oil
200ml white wine
1 lemon, cut into wedges

Preheat the oven to 180°C.

Gut and clean the trout, leaving the head on. Season on the outside and inside the belly with horopito pepper and salt. Place the onion halves in the stomach of the trout and poke skewers through one side of the belly into the onion and out the other side of the belly. Position the trout in the baking dish belly side down.

In a large bowl mix the garlic, vegetables and basil. Season with salt and pepper. Place the vegetables around the trout.

Dot the butter on the vegetables, drizzle the oil and wine over the trout and cover with aluminium foil. Place in the oven and bake for 20 minutes.

Serve on a platter garnished with lemon wedges.

Poking skewers through the trout's belly will help to keep the fish upright in the oven and make it easier to lift out whole and directly onto a serving platter when cooked.

TROUT CEVICHE Serves 6 as an entrée

1 x 2kg trout
juice of 1 lemon
salt and freshly ground black pepper
1 onion, finely diced
1 cup coconut cream
2 tomatoes, diced
2 tablespoons chopped parsley
2 spring onions, sliced

Remove the fillets from both sides of the trout and carefully remove the skin with a sharp filleting knife.

Remove the centre bone and any pin bones from the flesh. Cut into 3cm cubes and place in a bowl.

Drizzle lemon juice over the trout and season with salt and pepper. Set aside to marinate for 1 hour.

Add the onion, coconut cream and tomatoes to the trout, and mix thoroughly. Garnish with the parsley and spring onions.

Check the seasoning again and chill before serving.

POACHED TROUT ON MEDITERRANEAN CHARRED VEGETABLES Serves 6

FISH STOCK

2 fish heads and carcasses

4 litres water

1 bouquet garni

1 bay leaf

2 slices lemon

1 teaspoon black peppercorns

MEDITERRANEAN VEGETABLES

3 bulbs garlic

3 red onions, quartered

extra virgin olive oil for drizzling

salt and freshly ground black pepper

3 green capsicums

3 red capsicums

4 courgettes, sliced lengthways

1 eggplant, sliced lengthways

2 tablespoons capers

1 x 2.5kg trout

lemon wedges for garnishing

a few sprigs of rosemary
  for garnishing

For the fish stock, clean the fish heads and carcasses, and place in a large saucepan with the water. Add the bouquet garni, bay leaf, lemon slices and black peppercorns. Bring to the boil and simmer, skimming the surface occasionally, until reduced by half. Strain and set aside.

Preheat the oven to 180°C. Place the garlic bulbs and onion quarters in a baking dish, drizzle with olive oil, season with salt and cracked pepper, and roast in the oven for 10 minutes. Separate the garlic cloves, peel and chop. Place in a bowl with the onion.

Brush the capsicums with olive oil and char-grill on a barbecue or grill plate until the skin turns black. Remove the skin, halve the capsicums, remove the seeds, slice and place in the bowl. Brush the courgettes and eggplant with olive oil, and char-grill. Add these to the bowl with the capers. Season with salt, pepper and extra virgin olive oil.

Prepare and fillet the trout into even portions, leaving the skin on. Remove the pin bones using long-nosed pliers. Reheat the stock until simmering gently. Add the trout skin side down and poach until just cooked.

Arrange the vegetables on serving plates and carefully place the trout fillets on top. Garnish with lemon wedges and rosemary.

A good stock is essential for poaching trout to complement the flavour of the fish.

CAJUN-SPICED TROUT STEAKS ON CHERRY TOMATOES & SPINACH WITH GARLIC FRESHWATER CRAYFISH

Serves 6

1 large whole trout
2 tablespoons Cajun spice
olive oil for drizzling
12 freshwater crayfish
2 tablespoons butter
2 tablespoons crushed garlic
2 tablespoons olive oil
1 red onion, diced
¼ cup chopped fresh basil
½ cup canned Italian tomatoes, diced
12 cherry tomatoes
1 bunch spinach, washed and chopped
salt and freshly ground black pepper
1 spring onion, sliced for garnishing
2 tablespoons chopped parsley
 for garnishing

Preheat the grill. Clean and gut the trout and slice into 6 steaks, then season with the Cajun spice. Sprinkle a little olive oil over the trout, place in a baking dish and grill both sides until cooked. Keep warm.

Boil the crayfish in a saucepan of salted water for 5 minutes. Drain, then add the butter and 1 tablespoon of the garlic. Toss until well coated.

Heat the olive oil in a saucepan, add the red onion, remaining garlic, basil, Italian tomatoes and cherry tomatoes. Fold in the spinach leaves. Season to taste. Fry gently for 5 minutes.

Serve each steak on a bed of vegetables, top with two crayfish, and garnish with spring onion and parsley.

Freshwater crayfish can be cooked in the same way as large prawns. There are plenty of sweet juices under the head shell, but the small black gut-bag needs to be removed first as it is really sour.

BAKED BROWN TROUT FILLETS Serves 4

4 fillets brown trout, skin on
salt and freshly ground black pepper
3 cloves garlic, sliced
1 red onion, finely sliced
1 brown onion, finely sliced
2 tomatoes, sliced
1 green capsicum, deseeded and sliced
olive oil for drizzling
soya bean oil for drizzling
3 tablespoons butter

Season the fillets with salt and lots of ground pepper. Pierce the skin side of each fillet several times and push a garlic sliver into each cut.

Tear 4 pieces of aluminium foil large enough to wrap each fillet. Place 3 rings each of red and brown onion into the centre of each piece of foil, 2 slices of tomato, 2 slices of capsicum, a little salt and pepper and a touch of olive oil.

Place each fillet on the vegetables flesh-side down. Drizzle some more olive oil and soya bean oil on top. Finish with a knob of butter.

Fold the foil over and completely seal the parcel so no air can escape.

Place the parcels in a heavy-based baking dish directly over hot coals or rocks for 15–20 minutes. You can also cook the parcels on a barbecue or bake them in the oven. Serve the parcels sealed for opening at the table.

I use brown trout in this recipe as the flesh is firm and has a coarse texture. The French term *en papillote* is applied to this style of cooking where the food is sealed in a parcel. It keeps the fish fillets moist and juicy.

SMOKED BASIL PESTO TROUT & SMOKED TROUT EGGS ON PANCAKES
Serves 8

2 large whole trout
100ml malt vinegar
salt
200g basil pesto
200g sweet chilli sauce
2 strips trout roe

manuka sawdust

PANCAKES
2 eggs
2 cups flour
¼ cup sugar
1 tablespoon baking powder
1 teaspoon horopito pepper
pinch of salt
1 cup milk
butter for frying

mesclun to serve

Split open both trout through the back. Remove the stomach and blood vein and discard.

Brush the vinegar over the flesh of the trout, then sprinkle liberally with salt. Spread pesto on the flesh of one trout and sweet chilli sauce on the other.

Salt the trout roe all over. Place the trout on a wire rack to dry for 1 hour. This prevents the trout sticking to the wire smoking rack.

Prepare the smoker using manuka sawdust. Place the wire rack, trout and trout roe in the smoker. Cook for 25 minutes with hot, fast smoke.

For the pancakes, mix all the ingredients together. Ladle tablespoonfuls into a hot, buttered frying pan. Cook on both sides until golden.

To serve, place a little salad on each pancake and top with smoked trout and a piece of smoked trout roe. Serve hot or cold.

For me, hot-smoking trout is the only way to go because, honestly, I can't wait to eat it. Although I do remember the time I tasted the best-ever cold-smoked trout prepared by an old fishing mate who took all day to slowly smoke his trout. The flesh was so moist and soft I could eat two whole trout on my own. If you have the patience, try both ways and see which one you prefer. You will notice the difference.

SMOKED EEL PÂTÉ WITH
HOROPITO PARAOA PARAI Serves 8

SMOKED EEL PÂTÉ
1 cup flaked smoked eel
500g cream cheese, softened
100g butter, softened
2 tablespoons balsamic vinegar
1 tablespoon lemon juice
½ onion, minced
1 small clove garlic, minced
salt and freshly ground black pepper
chopped chives for garnishing
caviar for garnishing (optional)

HOROPITO PARAOA PARAI
3 ½ cups self-raising flour
½ teaspoon salt
1 tablespoon horopito pepper
cold water

extra virgin olive oil for frying

Place all the pâté ingredients, except the chives and caviar, in a blender and pulse until mixed well but not completely puréed. Place in a serving dish and refrigerate.

For the paraoa parai, place the flour, salt and horopito pepper in a large bowl. Using a wooden spoon, gradually mix in enough cold water to form a soft dough. Do not overmix; the dough should be light and fluffy.

Turn out the dough onto a lightly floured surface and roll out into a long tube, then cut into 5cm pieces.

Heat some oil in a frying pan and fry the pieces of dough in batches until golden on both sides. Place on absorbent kitchen paper.

Fill a piping bag with the pâté. Cut the fried bread in half and pipe some pâté on each half, then garnish with chives and caviar, if using.

For fried bread, the trick is to fry it quickly. The hotter the oil, the less time it takes to cook so it will absorb less fat and result in a lighter texture. I know some people would prefer using dripping but a healthier option is to use canola oil for deep-frying.

FRIED EEL STEAKS WITH SUNDRIED TOMATO PROVENÇALE & SMOKED EEL CAKES Serves 6

2 tablespoons olive oil, plus extra
  for frying
½ red onion, diced
50g sundried tomatoes
1 tomato, diced
1 tablespoon capers
6 pitted black olives
1 teaspoon crushed garlic
100ml tomato juice
salt and freshly ground black pepper
6 x 150g eel steaks
salad leaves to serve

SMOKED EEL CAKES
300g smoked eel
1 teaspoon crushed garlic
1 teaspoon grated ginger
1 teaspoon ground coriander
½ teaspoon crushed fresh chilli
salt and freshly ground black pepper
½ cup rice flour
2 spring onions, finely chopped
¾ cup dried breadcrumbs
3 tablespoons olive oil

Heat the olive oil in a frying pan, add the onion and sauté a little, then add the sundried tomatoes, fresh tomato, capers, olives and garlic. Pour in the tomato juice and simmer until reduced by half. Season to taste.

Season the eel steaks with a little salt and plenty of ground pepper. Heat a grill plate or frying pan, brush with olive oil and grill for 5 minutes on each side or until cooked through. Set aside. Keep warm.

For the smoked eel cakes, place the smoked eel, garlic, ginger, ground coriander and chilli in the bowl of a food processor. Blend until a smooth consistency is reached. Season with salt and pepper and add the rice flour and spring onions. Mix until smooth. Form into small cakes then roll in the breadcrumbs to coat.

Heat the oil in a frying pan, add the eel cakes and cook for 2–3 minutes on each side until golden brown. Serve the eel steaks and cakes on a bed of salad, and pour the sauce over.

When eeling with a hinaki (eel trap), always check the hinaki first thing in the morning. Eels will find a way out eventually if the hinaki is left too long in the stream.

STEAMED WHOLE EEL IN BLACK BEAN SAUCE Serves 4

1 whole eel

MARINADE
1 tablespoon light soy sauce
1 tablespoon sugar
½ tablespoon salt
½ tablespoon cornflour
1 tablespoon finely chopped ginger
2 tablespoons olive oil

2 spring onions, sliced for garnishing

BLACK BEAN SAUCE
2 tablespoons olive oil
½ red capsicum, cored, deseeded and diced
2 tablespoons finely chopped garlic
3 tablespoons black bean sauce
½ tablespoon salt
1 tablespoon sugar
1 tablespoon dark soy sauce
1 tablespoon cornflour
100ml water

Clean the eel with hot water, scraping off the slime carefully. Then, using a sharp knife, make 5cm-apart incisions through to the bone, around the width of the eel from head to tail.

For the marinade, mix all the ingredients together and marinate the eel, including the head, for 10 minutes.

Place the eel in a flat-bottomed steaming container, coiling the body to fit with the head in the centre. Steam gently until the skin starts to peel away from the flesh.

To make the sauce, heat the oil in a wok, add the capsicum, garlic and black bean sauce and stir-fry for 5 minutes to cook the capsicum and garlic. Add the remaining sauce ingredients and simmer for 10 minutes until the sauce thickens slightly.

Chop the eel into sections where it has already been cut, spoon on some sauce and garnish with the chopped spring onions.

Boiling and smoking are the most common cooking methods for eel. But try marinating the eel first, then finishing it off in a steamer. Use smaller eels for maximum flavour and better control of cooking time.

SMOKED WHITEBAIT, OLIVE & MACADAMIA OMELETTE Serves 1

200g whitebait
1 cup dried olive tree leaves or
  manuka sawdust
2 eggs
1 tablespoon cream
salt and freshly ground black pepper
15g butter
1 teaspoon pitted and diced black olives
2 teaspoons chopped macadamia nuts
fresh bread to serve
lemon wedges to serve
salad greens to serve

Place half the whitebait in a sieve. Sprinkle the olive leaves or manuka into a heavy-based saucepan, then place over a medium heat until the leaves start to smoke. Place the sieve of whitebait on the saucepan, cover with a lid and gently smoke for 10-15 minutes, stirring the whitebait regularly.

In a small bowl whisk together the eggs and cream, season with a little salt and pepper and stir in the remaining whitebait.

Heat an omelette pan or small non-stick frying pan. When hot, add the butter. It should sizzle and froth, but not burn.

Pour in the egg mixture and gently move it around a little with a fork. Lift the edges as they set to let the uncooked egg run underneath. When the egg has nearly set and the whitebait is cooked – it will turn from clear to white – turn the omelette over and cook for another 30 seconds.

When the omelette is ready, place the smoked whitebait along the centre and sprinkle with olives and macadamia nuts. Fold in half and serve with fresh bread, lemon wedges and salad.

WHITEBAIT ON SPINACH & POTATO NESTS Serves 4

2 large potatoes, peeled
2 litres canola oil
50ml extra virgin olive oil
¼ cup diced onion
¼ cup chopped rindless bacon
3 bunches spinach, washed, stalks
 discarded and leaves roughly torn
100ml balsamic vinegar
1kg whitebait
1 teaspoon crushed garlic
pinch of sea salt
pinch of white pepper
lemon wedges and fresh coriander
 for garnishing

Thinly slice the potato and cut into matchsticks. Heat the canola oil in a deep-fryer to 180°C. Place the potato in a small sieve and press down with another sieve or large ladle to create the shape of a nest. Place sieve carefully in the hot oil and cook until golden brown. Remove the potato nest from the sieve carefully and place on absorbent kitchen paper to soak up the remaining oil.

Heat a little olive oil in a frying pan, add the onion and bacon and sauté for 2 minutes. Add the spinach leaves and toss through until warm. Sprinkle the balsamic vinegar over and fold into the ingredients. Arrange on 4 serving plates and place a potato nest on top of each serving.

Heat the remaining olive oil in a frying pan. Toss the whitebait in the oil, then add the garlic, salt and white pepper. Fry for 1 minute and spoon into the potato nests. Garnish with lemon wedges and fresh coriander.

I have been so fortunate living in the Bay of Plenty. For me it's a resourceful area that has much to offer – forests and native bush with excellent hunting spots, lakes and rivers offering spectacular trout fishing and, just around the corner, the sunny east coast where you can find mussels, kina or perhaps a crayfish if you're lucky. The 'Bay of Plenty' says it all!

Half an hour from home there's a small coastal town called Maketu. It's a place my family and I regularly visit when it's time to change our diet from meat to seafood. During the warm summer periods you'll catch us splashing for flounder or gathering pipi and cockles in the estuary. Whenever we head to the beach, harvesting seafood comes first before kicking back. Nothing can beat fresh pipi and yellow belly flounder straight off the barbecue.

As the weather warms up the hunting is put on hold for a little while – away with the rifle and out with the scuba gear. Just one phone call and, before you know it, we're heading to our favourite marks along the east coast.

Hunting for food underwater is a totally different ball game to taking a rifle into the thick bush and scrub of Tane Mahuta. Almost nothing gives me more pleasure than donning my mask and flippers and diving to explore the rocky crevices and kelp fields of Tangaroa.

Next time you find a secret stash of seafood while at the beach or if one of the cuzzies drops off a fat mussel bag or cray, try these tasty recipes. Enjoy!

SEASHORE
TAKUTAI MOANA

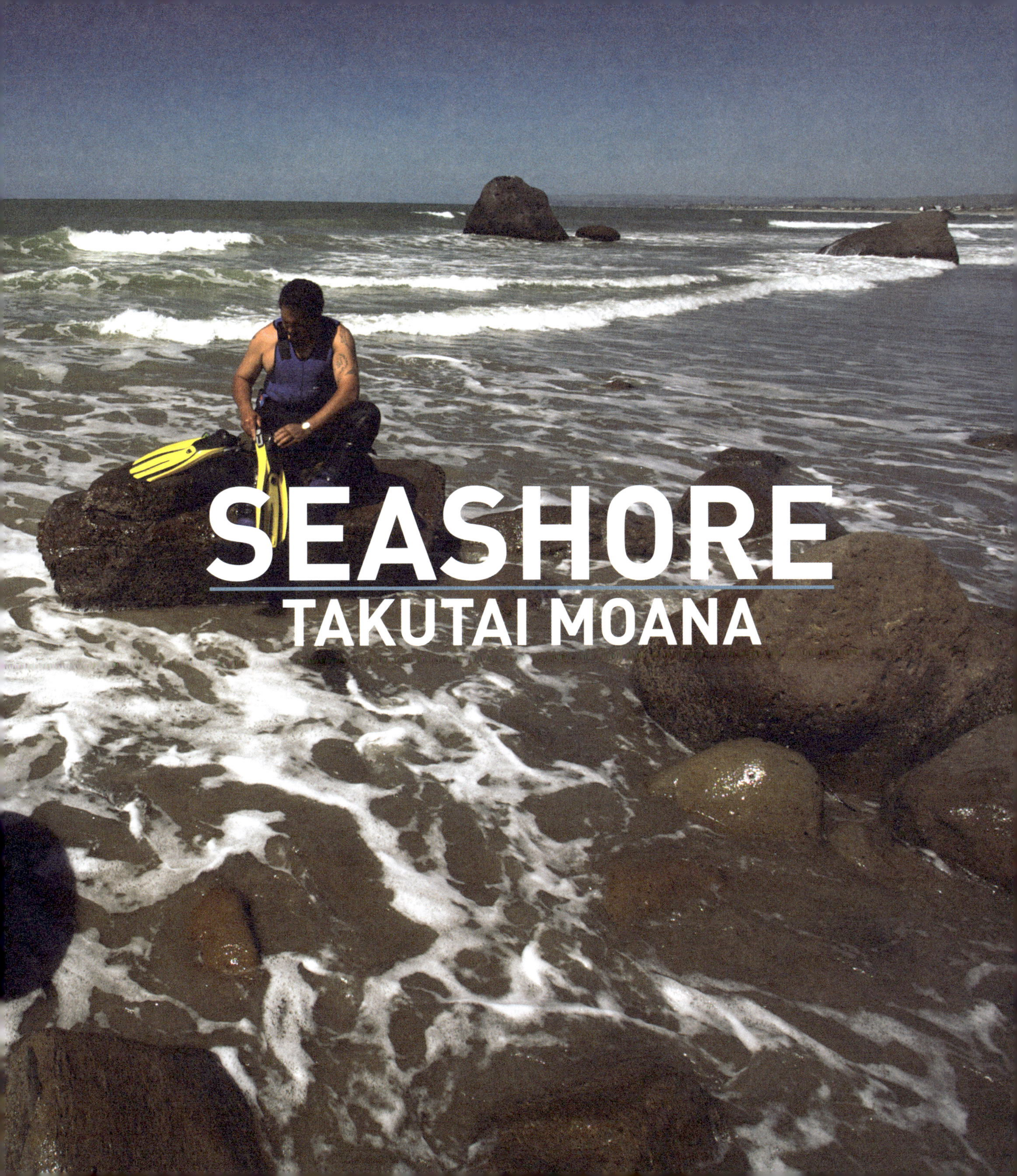

PARENGO & AVOCADO SALAD WITH
GAZPACHO SAUCE Serves 2

2 red capsicums
1 x 200g piece of parengo, sliced
100g butter
½ ripe avocado, cut into small cubes
100ml olive oil
1 tablespoon chopped chives
1 tablespoon lime juice
1 fresh red chilli, seeds removed,
  finely chopped
salt and freshly ground black pepper
sour cream to serve

GAZPACHO SAUCE
½ small onion, minced
½ cup diced tomatoes
¼ green capsicum, cored, deseeded
  and chopped
1 teaspoon honey
¼ cucumber, peeled, seeds removed
  and diced
juice of 1 lemon
1 tablespoon wine vinegar
4 basil leaves
pinch of ground cumin
dash of Tabasco sauce
1 tablespoon olive oil
1 cup chilled tomato juice
salt and freshly ground black pepper

Grill the red capsicum until soft and the skin is slightly blackened, then remove the skin and seeds. Open out and cut 4 rounds of flesh into 6cm circles. Bake the parengo in a little butter for 1½ hours at 180°C. Set aside to cool.

Mix the avocado with half the parengo, the olive oil, chives, lime juice, and chilli to produce a zesty, guacamole-type sauce. Season to taste.

Place a layer of the grilled capsicum, avocado sauce and the rest of the parengo into a 6cm stainless steel ring on a plate to form a tower. Finish with a layer of capsicum. Repeat with remaining ingredients to make a second tower then refrigerate.

For the gazpacho sauce, process all the ingredients except the tomato juice in a food processor, then combine the mixture with the tomato juice in a large bowl. Season to taste, cover and chill.

Remove the ring from the parengo and avocado, pour the gazpacho sauce around the side and top with a good dollop of sour cream.

BAKED AVOCADO WITH SWEET CHILLI SURIMI & HOLLANDAISE SAUCE Serves 4 as an entrée

½ red onion, diced
3 tablespoons olive oil
1 cup surimi
1 spring onion, finely sliced
4 tablespoons sweet chilli sauce
chopped parsley
2 avocados, halved and stones
  removed

HOLLANDAISE SAUCE
4 egg yolks
50ml white wine vinegar
salt and freshly ground black pepper
100g butter, melted

Preheat the oven to 180°C. Sweat the onion and olive oil in a hot frying pan. Add the surimi and toss, then add the spring onion, sweet chilli sauce and parsley.

Spoon the surimi mixture into the avocado halves, place in an oven dish and bake for 10-15 minutes.

For the hollandaise sauce, put the egg yolks, vinegar and seasoning in a stainless steel bowl and whisk over a saucepan of boiling water until the mixture thickens without curdling. Pour in the melted butter, a little at a time, while whisking continuously until it reaches the ribbon stage (the mixture forms a ribbon on the surface when it falls from the whisk).

Remove the avocados from the oven and spoon some hollandaise over the top of each. Turn the oven to grill and slightly brown the hollandaise. Serve immediately.

BEER-BATTERED PACIFIC OYSTERS WITH DIPPING SAUCE Serves 2

DIPPING SAUCE
¼ red onion, diced
½ spring onion, sliced
1 teaspoon brown sugar
1 teaspoon crushed ginger
1 teaspoon crushed garlic
2 tablespoons sweet chilli sauce
100ml lime cordial
2 tablespoons fish sauce
2 tablespoons soy sauce
4 tablespoons extra virgin olive oil

BEER-BATTERED OYSTERS
2 litres canola oil
2½ cups flour
1 can beer
2 tablespoons chopped parsley
salt and freshly ground black pepper
12 Pacific oysters

For the dipping sauce, mix all the ingredients together and set aside.

For the oysters, heat the canola oil to 180°C. Mix together 2 cups of the flour and the beer to a smooth consistency then fold in the parsley and season with salt and pepper.

Shell the oysters and pat dry with a tea towel or absorbent kitchen paper. Lightly coat with the remaining flour, then dip in the batter and deep-fry in the hot oil until golden. Serve immediately with the dipping sauce.

Try to avoid dark, strong-flavoured beer when making batter for oysters so as not to overpower the delicate taste. Lightly coat the oysters with the batter so they cook quickly and retain as much of their juice as possible.

For variation, drizzle the dipping sauce over some of the raw oysters while still in their half shell, as in the photograph (right).

SPICY NOODLE & TUATUA SOUP
Serves 4

1 teaspoon peanut oil
1 large onion, finely chopped
2 cloves garlic, finely chopped
1½ teaspoons chopped ginger
1 red chilli, deseeded and sliced
2 tablespoons dark soy sauce
1 tablespoon black bean sauce
12 tuatua
1.25 litres chicken stock
200g rice vermicelli noodles
2 eggs, beaten
¼ cucumber, peeled and seeds removed,
  thinly sliced lengthways
50g snowpea shoots or bean sprouts
2 spring onions, thinly sliced

Heat the oil in a wok or large saucepan until medium-hot. Stir-fry the onion and garlic until tender, stirring frequently (around 3 minutes). Add the ginger and stir-fry for a further 2 minutes, then add the chilli and toss for a further 20–30 seconds.

Add the soy sauce and the black bean sauce. Reduce the heat slightly and simmer for 1 minute. Remove the tuatua flesh from the shells, add to the pan and simmer gently until cooked (around 1½ minutes). Remove from the heat.

In a separate saucepan bring the chicken stock to the boil, then take off the heat. Cut the noodles with scissors for easier handling when serving, then add to the stock. Set aside.

Heat a small non-stick frying pan and pour in the eggs. Cook on both sides until set, then chop into thin strips.

Pour the noodles and stock into the wok and mix well. Divide the egg, cucumber, pea shoots or bean sprouts and spring onions evenly between 4 deep soup bowls, then pour over the soup and serve.

This noodle soup is my version of a popular dish from Singapore, which uses prawns instead of tuatua. It is traditionally eaten with a fork and spoon.

To make a lighter meal you can omit the eggs without spoiling the dish. Stir-fried broccoli or Chinese cabbage is another tasty addition.

This is a great soup for using cheap fish fillets. Some packets of Asian noodles have spices and seasonings that are fine to add to this dish.

PIPI & SCALLOP SPAGHETTI Serves 4

olive oil for frying
1 onion, finely diced
1 garlic clove, finely chopped
100ml white wine
grated zest of 1 orange
1 cup orange juice
grated zest of 1 lemon
grated zest of 1 lime
½ cup cream
segments of 1 orange with membranes
  removed
1 tablespoon chopped chives,
  plus extra for garnishing
400g fresh spaghetti
12 pipi
250g scallops
salt and freshly ground black pepper
lemon wedges and chopped chives
  for garnishing

In a frying pan heat some olive oil, add the onion and garlic, and sauté for 1 minute. Add the white wine, orange zest and juice, and the lemon and lime zest. Simmer to reduce slightly then add the cream, orange segments and chives and simmer for 6 minutes.

Meanwhile, bring a large saucepan of well-salted water to the boil, add the spaghetti and boil until al dente (firm to the bite). Drain.

Add the pipi to the frying pan and simmer until their shells open. Add the scallops and sauté for a further 5 minutes. Season with salt and pepper.

Add the spaghetti to the pan and toss gently. Divide among 4 plates. Garnish with lemon wedges, chives and remaining sauce.

To remove sand from inside the pipi, cover the shellfish with fresh seawater prior to cooking and leave to soak for a few hours. The pipi will eventually spit out the sand.

GREEN-LIPPED MUSSELS FILLED WITH BASIL PESTO STUFFING & SPICY TOMATO MORNAY Serves 2

10 large mussels
1 litre milk
1 small onion, peeled and finely diced
4 cloves
50g butter
50g flour
1 tablespoon tomato purée
½ cup grated tasty cheese (optional)
1 teaspoon crushed fresh chilli
salt and freshly ground black pepper

BASIL PESTO STUFFING
½ cup pine nuts
½ cup grated parmesan
¼ cup basil leaves
2 cloves garlic, crushed
1 cup fresh breadcrumbs
100ml olive oil

Wash and shell one side only of the mussels. Place in a hot frying pan, shell side down for 5 minutes.

Heat the milk in a saucepan with the onion and cloves to boiling point. In a separate saucepan melt the butter, add the flour and stir over a medium heat for 2 minutes. Slowly add the milk, stirring continuously, until the sauce coats the back of the spoon. Stir in the tomato purée, cheese (if using) and chilli. Season to taste.

For the pesto, place all the ingredients in a blender or food processor and pulse to combine. Fill the mussels with the pesto stuffing and place in an ovenproof dish. Spoon the tomato mornay over the mussels and grill until golden. Serve hot.

Always check that mussels are fresh when buying from the supermarket. Any mussel that is already open has died and should be avoided.

MUSSEL TOROI Serves 4

1 bunch watercress or puha,
 well washed
salt
12 mussels, shelled

Boil the watercress or puha in salted water for
10 minutes. Strain.

Chop the mussels into small pieces and boil in
hot water for 10 minutes.

Add the watercress or puha to the mussels and cook
for a further 20 minutes.

Allow to cool in the mussel juices, then place in
airtight jars and refrigerate. This will keep in
the refrigerator for up to 2 weeks. Serve as a soup
alongside your favourite steak.

When buying mussels for toroi, make sure
they are the freshest available. Collecting
your own is even better.

Pikopiko or turnip-tops can be used in
place of watercress and puha if desired for
a variation in taste and texture. An extra
10 minutes cooking time will be necessary
for the pikopiko, however.

CRAYFISH BISQUE Serves 4

1 fresh 600–800g crayfish
1 onion, diced
1 carrot, sliced
1 stalk celery, sliced
100g butter
100g flour
2 tablespoons tomato paste
100ml brandy
2 drops Tabasco sauce
100ml cream
salt and freshly ground black pepper
chopped parsley for garnishing

Bring a large saucepan of salted water (around 2 litres) to the boil. Add the crayfish and simmer for 10 minutes. Remove the crayfish and reserve the stock. Take the meat out of the crayfish tail, remove and discard the vein, and dice the meat into 1cm pieces. Reserve the legs for garnishing.

In a large saucepan fry the onion, carrot and celery in the butter. Add the flour and tomato paste, mix well then add the brandy and 1 litre of hot crayfish stock (reserving the rest of the stock for another use). Stir until well combined.

Bring to the boil, stirring, and simmer for 30 minutes. Add the Tabasco and cream and season to taste.

Serve the bisque in soup bowls, divide the crayfish meat among the bowls and garnish with chopped parsley.

CRAYFISH MORNAY Serves 4 as an entrée

1 x 600g cooked crayfish
30g butter
30g flour
1 cup milk, warmed
½ cup grated colby cheese
100ml olive oil
1 onion, finely diced
salt and freshly ground black pepper
mashed potato
chopped parsley for garnishing
1 lemon, cut into wedges

Separate the tail and head from the crayfish, remove the meat from the tail, reserving the shell, and dice finely.

Melt the butter in a saucepan, add the flour and cook for 2 minutes, stirring continuously. Add the warm milk a little at a time and stir until the sauce is smooth. Fold in the cheese and remove from the heat.

Heat the olive oil in a frying pan and fry the crayfish flesh and the onion until the onion is soft. Fold the cheese sauce into the mixture and season to taste.

Place the mashed potato down the middle of a plate. Arrange the crayfish body and head upside down in the middle of the potato. Fill the head with lemon wedges.

Fill the tail shell with mornay sauce and sprinkle with a little chopped parsley. Grill until golden brown, then place beside the crayfish torso. It should now look like an intact crayfish. Serve immediately.

SALMON & PAUA OMELETTE WITH CITRUS AVOCADO OIL Serves 2

butter and extra virgin olive oil
 for frying
100g fresh salmon, diced
¼ onion, diced
100g paua, sliced
2 tablespoons cream
salt and freshly ground black pepper
4 eggs
50ml milk
30g snowpea shoots
chopped chives

CITRUS AVOCADO OIL
4 tablespoons avocado oil
4 tablespoons fresh orange juice
3 tablespoons lemon juice
1 tablespoon honey
salt and freshly ground black pepper

For the citrus avocado oil, shake all the ingredients together in a jar and leave to stand for 30 minutes.

Place some butter and olive oil in a frying pan and sauté the salmon pieces until just cooked, then remove and set aside. Add some more butter to the pan and fry the onion and paua. Add the cream and season to taste. Simmer to reduce slightly. Remove from heat.

Lightly beat the eggs and milk until just combined. Season with salt and pepper. Heat a non-stick frying pan over a medium heat. Add some oil and butter, then pour in the egg mixture. Use a wooden spoon to pull the egg from the sides into the centre as it sets.

While the omelette is still slightly runny on top evenly distribute the salmon and creamed paua over it then sprinkle the snowpea shoots and chives across the centre. Fold the omelette in half and slide onto a plate. Drizzle with a little citrus avocado oil.

To make a puffy omelette, fry the salmon and paua as normal then mix them both together in a frying pan. Pour in the whisked egg mixture, stir until combined and place under a grill.

The citrus avocado oil is also great for drizzling over leafy greens.

PAUA WITH MOZZARELLA, TOMATO & BASIL SALAD Serves 4

4 paua
6 eggs
salt and freshly ground black pepper
2 cups breadcrumbs
2 tablespoons garlic flakes
2 tablespoons dried parsley
4 thin slices tasty cheese
4 slices sandwich ham
flour for dusting
1 litre canola oil
150g bocconcini or fresh mozzarella, drained and thinly sliced
4 tomatoes, sliced
12–18 fresh basil leaves
Maldon sea salt
60ml extra virgin olive oil
splash of balsamic vinegar

Wrap the paua in a tea towel and tenderise using a hammer or meat tenderiser.

Mix the eggs, salt and pepper in a bowl with a little water. In another bowl mix the breadcrumbs, garlic flakes and dried parsley.

Place a slice of cheese and ham on top of each paua and hold together with toothpicks. Dust the paua in a little flour, then dip in the egg wash and roll in the breadcrumb mixture. Heat the oil in a large frying pan and deep-fry the paua until light brown on both sides. Remove and place on absorbent kitchen paper.

Arrange the slices of mozzarella, tomatoes and whole basil leaves over 4 serving plates. Sprinkle the Maldon sea salt over the tomatoes.

Just before serving drizzle with extra olive oil and a little balsamic vinegar. Finish with a generous grind of pepper. Remove the toothpicks from the paua, cut each paua in half and serve 2 halves on each portion of salad.

Before entering the water to gather kai a karakia or prayer is always said for a safe passage, an abundant catch, a safe return and to respect the gods.

PAUA THREE WAYS Serves 4 as an entrée

CREAMED PAUA

2 tablespoons butter

1 onion, finely diced

1 clove garlic, chopped

2 paua, sliced

250ml cream

salt and freshly ground black pepper

2 paua shells to serve

CURRIED PAUA

2 tablespoons olive oil

1 red onion, finely diced

1 teaspoon curry powder

2 paua, sliced

1 can coconut cream

salt and freshly ground black pepper

2 paua shells to serve

SPICY PAUA

2 tablespoons olive oil

1 each red and yellow capsicums,
  cored, deseeded and sliced

1 spring onion, sliced

2 paua, sliced

½ fresh red chilli, deseeded and
  chopped

1 clove garlic, chopped

4 tablespoons sweet chilli sauce

salt and freshly ground black pepper

2 paua shells to serve

fresh bread to serve

For the creamed paua, heat the butter in a frying pan and add the onion, garlic and paua. Fry over a medium heat for 2 minutes, then add the cream and simmer until the cream has reduced slightly and thickened. Season with salt and pepper. Serve hot inside paua shells.

For the curried paua, heat the olive oil in a frying pan and add the onion, curry powder and paua. Fry over a medium heat for 2 minutes, then add the coconut cream and simmer until the cream is reduced slightly and thickened. Season with salt and pepper. Serve hot inside paua shells.

For the spicy paua, heat the oil in a frying pan and add the capsicum, spring onion, paua, chilli and garlic, and sauté for 2 minutes. Add the chilli sauce. Season with salt and pepper. Serve hot inside paua shells.

Serve all 3 paua dishes together with fresh bread for a delicious paua feast.

When gathering kai moana only take what you need.

FLOUNDER CASSEROLE Serves 4

100g butter
olive oil for frying
1 onion, finely diced
1 carrot, finely diced
2 cloves garlic, crushed
1 red chilli, deseeded and
  finely chopped
¼ cup plain flour
1 litre tomato juice
4 tomatoes, chopped
1 courgette, chopped
1 tablespoon chopped fresh thyme
2 bay leaves
4 x 600g whole flounder
salt and freshly ground black pepper
8 small Maori potatoes, boiled

Heat the butter and a little olive oil in a saucepan. Add the onion, carrot, garlic and chilli, and sauté for 5 minutes.

Stir in the flour, then add the tomato juice. Mix well, then add the chopped tomatoes, courgette, thyme and bay leaves. Bring to the boil, then reduce to a simmer for 5 minutes.

Clean the flounder and score the flesh on each side a couple of times with a sharp knife. Season both sides with salt and pepper. Cut each flounder in half crossways and place in the tomato casserole, ensuring the fish is covered with the sauce. Place a lid on the saucepan and simmer for a further 10 minutes.

Dice the potatoes and mix into the casserole to warm through. Check that the fish is cooked, then serve hot.

In this recipe the flounder is poached in the casserole liquid. Make sure the flounder is just cooked so it holds its shape. If it is over-cooked, the fish will break up.

FLOUNDER MUSSEL WRAPS
Serves 4 as an entrée

2 x 800g whole flounder
salt and freshly ground black pepper
½ onion, diced
2 sprigs fresh thyme
2 sprigs parsley
1 bay leaf
6 peppercorns
8 green-lipped mussels
olive oil for frying
100ml dry white wine
100ml cream
10 grapes
2 teaspoons lime cordial
2 tablespoons chopped parsley,
  plus extra for garnishing
1 lemon, sliced
salt and freshly ground black pepper

Using a sharp filleting knife, follow down both sides of the backbone of each flounder and slice away the fillets. Repeat on the other side. Remove and discard skin from fillets. Season the fillets on both sides with salt and pepper.

Discard the stomachs, wash the flounder frames and chop into small pieces. Place frame pieces in a saucepan with enough water to cover. Add the onion, thyme, parsley, bay leaf and peppercorns. Bring to the boil, then simmer for 20 minutes.

Wash and shell the mussels, removing the beards. Roll each fillet around a mussel and secure with a toothpick. Heat a frying pan with a little olive oil and carefully sear the fillets for 1 minute on each side. Add the white wine and 1 litre of the strained fish stock and allow the wraps to poach for 5 minutes.

Remove the wraps and reduce the cooking liquid by half. Add the cream, grapes, lime cordial and a sprinkling of chopped parsley, and simmer to reduce the sauce by half again. Season to taste. Divide the lemon slices between the serving plates and place the flounder wraps on top. Pour the sauce over the top and garnish with chopped parsley.

Fillets from large flounder are better for rolling around the mussel flesh. The trick with this dish is to poach each wrap quickly for a softer texture.

Whenever I go diving with the whanau for kina and crayfish we always take a couple of fishing rods and lures – just in case we bump into a school of fish. Kahawai seem to be the most common fish along the east coast, all year round. The kahawai is an underrated fish that not too many people target. That's not the case for our waka! If we manage to catch a couple of kahawai, the diving is inevitably put on hold for at least an hour while we have a cook-up.

It's amazing to see a school of kahawai swimming and feeding. It creates a boiling effect along the surface of the water. If you know anything about sea fishing then you will probably know that below the school of kahawai lurk the darker shadows of larger fish like the kingfish, just waiting to prey on the smaller fish above. Catching a kingfish is well worth it if you know the right tactics and can spare some extra time.

My most educational deep-sea fishing experience has got to be a trip on a trawling boat off Tauranga. If you want to see hundreds of species of deep-sea fish caught and prepared for the market, then this is one way to learn about them and what they taste like. Half the species caught I had never seen before.

Fishing is great fun for the whole family – whether you are on a boat or fishing from the beach. When you do get lucky, remember the golden rule when cooking: don't overcook your fish!

Enjoy the spoils Tangaroa has to offer. Tight lines!

DEEP SEA

TE MOANA-NUI

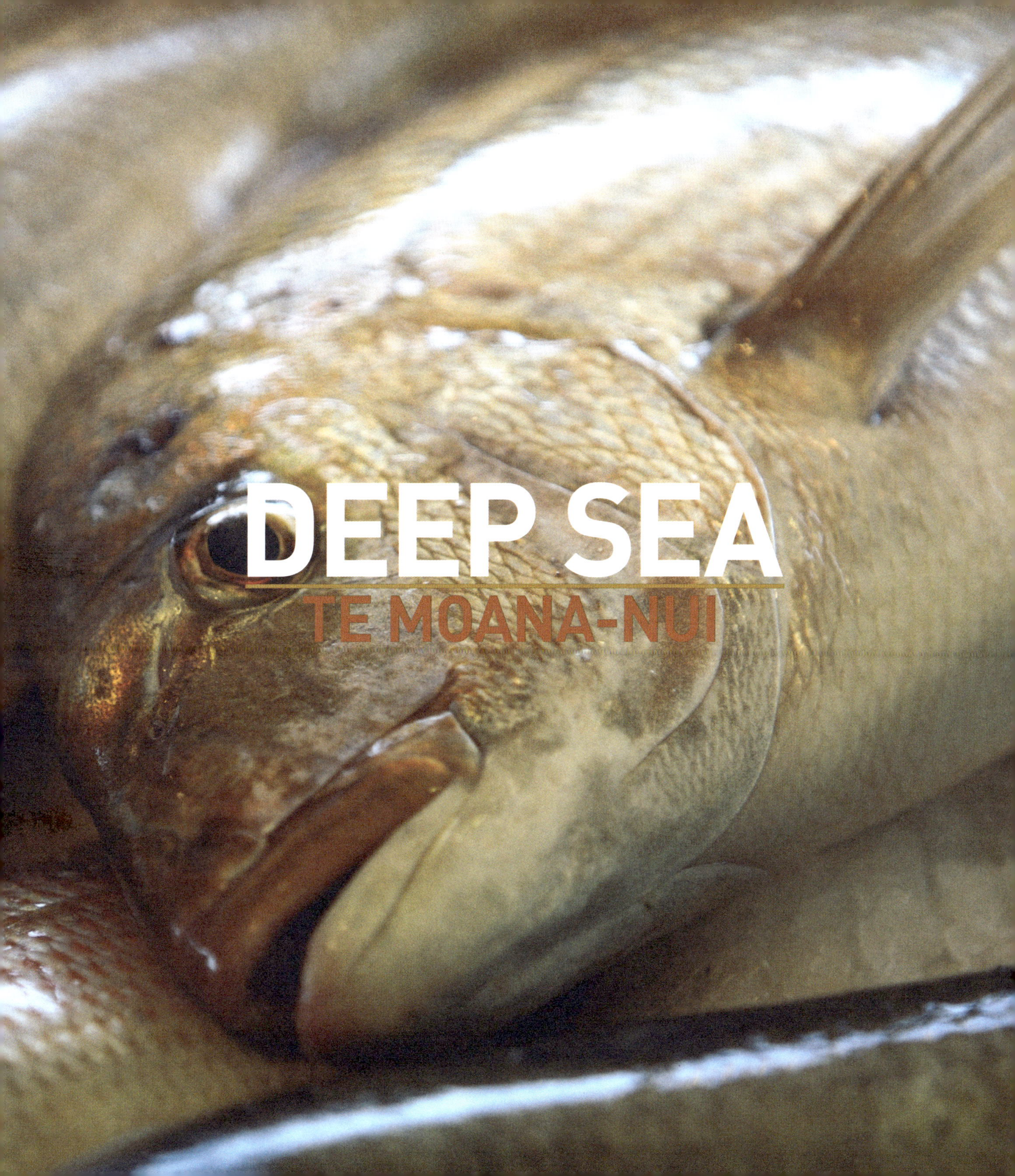

STIR-FRIED SCALLOPS
Serves 4 as an entrée

2 tablespoons olive or peanut oil
2 cloves garlic, finely sliced
1 tablespoon grated ginger
200g scallops
1 tablespoon dry sherry
¼ teaspoon sugar
100g snowpea shoots
1 tablespoon light soy sauce
6 button mushrooms, sliced
1 cup cooked rice to serve

Heat a wok and, just before it starts smoking, swirl in the oil. Stir in the garlic and ginger, and fry, stirring, for 30 seconds. Remove with a slotted spoon to a bowl and set aside.

Add the scallops to the wok and stir-fry for 2 minutes. Return the garlic and ginger to the wok along with the sherry, sugar, snowpea shoots, soy sauce and mushrooms. Stir-fry for 1 minute.

Divide the rice between 4 scallop shells and top with scallops.

Never throw the shells from shellfish back into the sea, especially near a popular kai moana bed.

CURRIED SCALLOPS
Serves 2 as an entrée

¼ cup honey
2 teaspoons curry powder
3 tablespoons Dijon mustard
1 teaspoon lemon juice
1 teaspoon white pepper
pinch of cinnamon
10 scallops in the shell

Combine all the ingredients except the scallops.

Remove the top half of the scallop shells, remove the gut bag and frill around each scallop, leaving it attached to the shell. Brush the scallops generously with the prepared curry mixture.

Place the scallops on a barbecue or in a large frying pan and heat until the juices from the scallops and the marinade start to bubble. Serve immediately. (Don't overcook the scallops or they will become rubbery.)

The golden rule when preparing scallops is to cook them quickly. They only need a little heat to warm through. Scallops can be eaten raw so avoid overcooking this delicacy from Tangaroa.

FRONT AND REAR: CURRIED SCALLOPS; CENTRE: STIR-FRIED SCALLOPS

BOTTLED TREVALLY Makes 1 x 500ml jar

600g trevally, scaled
½ teaspoon salt
1 tablespoon malt vinegar
1 tablespoon olive oil
4 tablespoons sweet chilli sauce

Remove the fillets from the trevally, leaving the skin on, and remove the pin bones and backbone.

Cut the trevally fillets into 6 portions and place inside a sterilised preserving jar with the skin side facing out. Fill the middle with smaller portions. Mix the salt, vinegar, olive oil and sweet chilli sauce together and pour into the jar over the fillets.

Ensure the rim is free from food so the jar seals properly then screw the lid on. Place the jar in a large saucepan of water and boil for 3 hours. Remove from the saucepan and set aside to cool. Store in the pantry until ready to use. The longer the jar is kept, the better the flavours and the bones become soft and edible. Once opened, store in the refrigerator for up to 10 days.

For flavour variations, try tomato pesto, sundried tomatoes, chives, wasabi or fresh herbs such as coriander, basil or thyme instead of sweet chilli sauce. Serve the trevally on toast with a touch of wasabi, or sprinkle pieces of the fish over a fresh summer salad or mix with pasta.

KAHAWAI CEVICHE
Serves 4 as an entrée

2 x 800g kahawai fillets, diced
1 tomato, diced
1 onion, finely diced
6 ice cubes
300ml water
salt and freshly ground black pepper

Place the kahawai in a bowl. Add the tomato and onion and season with salt and pepper. Add 6 ice cubes to 300ml of water and pour over the kahawai.

Allow to sit for 5 minutes. Season with salt and pepper. Serve immediately.

MUSSEL FRITTERS & SWORDFISH FILLETS WITH A CRAYFISH BEURRE BLANC Serves 4

COURT BOUILLON

2 litres water

2 sprigs parsley

6 black peppercorns

½ onion, sliced

2 bay leaves

1 carrot, peeled and chopped

1 crayfish tail

MUSSEL FRITTERS

1 cup plain flour

1 egg

1 cup milk

8 mussels

2 tablespoons chopped coriander

2 cloves garlic, crushed

salt and freshly ground black pepper

butter and olive oil for frying

4 x 150g swordfish fillets

BEURRE BLANC

½ onion, finely diced

4 tablespoons chopped fresh chervil

50ml white vine vinegar

100ml Sauvignon Blanc

350g butter, cubed

lemon wedges for garnishing

chervil sprigs for garnishing

For the court bouillon, combine the water, parsley, peppercorns, onion, bay leaves and carrot in a saucepan and bring to the boil. Reduce to a simmer, add the crayfish tail and cook for 10 minutes, then remove from the heat. When cool, remove the crayfish flesh from the shell, chop into small dice and set aside. Reserve the court bouillon.

For the mussel fritters, place the flour in a bowl then add the egg and milk. Whisk until smooth. Shell the mussels, chop into small pieces and add to the batter, then mix in the coriander, garlic, salt and pepper. Heat some butter and a little olive oil in a frying pan. Drop spoonfuls of mixture into the pan and fry on each side until golden. Remove from the pan and keep warm.

Refresh the pan with olive oil. Season the swordfish fillets and pan-fry for 3 minutes each side. Remove from the pan and keep warm.

For the beurre blanc, add 1 ladleful of court bouillon to the pan to deglaze. Add the onion, chervil, vinegar and wine. Return to the heat, bring to a simmer and reduce by half. Remove from the heat and add the butter, piece by piece, whisking continuously, until glossy. Strain the beurre blanc, then fold in the crayfish meat.

Place 2 mussel fritters in the centre of each of 4 plates, top with the swordfish and spoon the crayfish beurre blanc over the top. Garnish with lemon wedges and sprigs of chervil.

CHINESE TARAKIHI SOUP Serves 4

100ml olive oil

2 thumb-sized pieces ginger, peeled
  and crushed with the flat edge
  of a knife

500g fish bones

2 litres water

100g Chinese egg noodles

2 tarakihi fillets, thinly sliced

small piece fresh root ginger, peeled
  and finely sliced

2 spring onions, sliced

150g tofu, diced

1 carrot, sliced

½ stick celery, sliced

sea salt

garlic oil

handful coriander leaves, chopped

soy sauce and chopped fresh chillies
  to serve

Heat the olive oil in a saucepan. Fry the ginger and fish bones until fragrant. Add the water and bring to the boil. Reduce the heat, cover and simmer for 30 minutes, then leave to cool. Drain the stock and set aside.

Blanch the noodles in boiling water for 5 minutes. Drain and divide between 4 serving bowls.

Bring the fish stock to the boil. Add the tarakihi, ginger, spring onions, tofu, carrot and celery to the stock and boil for 2–3 minutes. Season with salt and pepper.

Pour into the bowls of noodles. Drizzle with garlic oil and sprinkle with coriander.

Serve with a small dish of chopped chillies and soy sauce for people to help themselves.

It is a Maori custom to throw back the first fish you catch. This will bring good luck, respect and a better catch next time.

STEAMED SNAPPER & VEGETABLES WITH FRIED POTATO MATCHSTICKS & TURMERIC CREAM SAUCE

Serves 2

1 red chilli, deseeded and
  finely chopped

3 cloves garlic, finely chopped

¼ cup chopped fresh coriander

2 teaspoons ground turmeric

salt and freshly ground black pepper

2 x 600g whole snapper, gutted
  and scaled

6 small broccoli florets

4 cauliflower florets

200g baby carrots

100g button mushrooms, quartered

12 asparagus spears

200ml soya bean oil

1 large potato, scrubbed and cut
  into matchsticks

TURMERIC CREAM SAUCE

½ onion, finely diced

1 teaspoon ground turmeric

olive oil for frying

100ml white wine

100ml cream

salt and freshly ground black pepper

In a bowl mix together the chilli, garlic, coriander, turmeric, salt and pepper. Rub this mixture over the snapper inside and out.

Place the broccoli, cauliflower, carrots, mushrooms and asparagus in the bottom layer of a steamer, season with salt and pepper then place the snapper in the top layer and steam for 10 minutes.

Heat the soya bean oil in a frying pan and fry the potato matchsticks until crisp, then drain on absorbent kitchen paper.

For the sauce, fry the onion and turmeric in a little olive oil for 1 minute until the onion is soft. Add the white wine, bring to a simmer and reduce by half. Add the cream, season to taste, then reduce until the sauce thickens a little.

Place the vegetables on a serving platter and top with the whole snapper. Pour the sauce over the fish and finish by sprinkling the potato matchsticks over the top.

Steaming helps prevent the snapper from falling apart. Make sure the snapper is just cooked in order for it to hold its shape.

ROASTED SNAPPER WITH
KINA SALSA VERDE Serves 2

KINA SALSA VERDE

2 mint leaves, chopped

2 tablespoons chopped fresh
 flat-leaf parsley

1½ tablespoons capers, chopped

2 kina roe segments, chopped

4 anchovy fillets, chopped

1 clove garlic, sliced

salt and freshly ground black pepper

ROASTED SNAPPER

2 tomatoes, sliced

1½ tablespoons capers

1 clove garlic, sliced

1 red chilli, deseeded and chopped

olive oil

200ml seafood stock

pinch of sea salt

2 x 250g snapper fillets, boned and
 with the skin on

4 kina roe segments

salt and freshly ground black pepper

chopped fresh thyme

To make the kina salsa verde, combine all the ingredients in a small bowl. Mix well and set aside.

For the roasted snapper, preheat the oven to 220°C. Line the base of a baking dish with non-stick baking paper. Place the sliced tomatoes on the baking paper and sprinkle with capers, garlic, chilli, olive oil, seafood stock and salt.

Brush the skin side of the first snapper fillet with some olive oil and place skin side down on the tomatoes. Season with a little salt and pepper then spread the salsa verde over the fillet. Place the kina roe segments on top.

Season the flesh side of the second snapper fillet and place flesh side down on top of the first one. Brush the fillet with oil, and season with salt and thyme.

Roast the fish for 20 minutes until just cooked. Cut the snapper stack in half on an angle and serve on top of the kina salsa. Drizzle with cooking juices and serve.

Be careful when seasoning this dish with salt as capers and anchovies are also salty and help to season the snapper.

I have noticed that when you find kina scattered throughout rocks they are fatter than kina from a large group feeding in one area.

GRILLED KINGFISH STEAKS ON WARM NIÇOISE SALAD WITH CAPER AÏOLI

Serves 4

NIÇOISE SALAD
100ml olive oil, plus extra for drizzling
100g green beans, sliced
1 red onion, finely diced
1 red capsicum, cored, deseeded
  and diced
1 green capsicum, cored, deseeded
  and diced
1 yellow capsicum, cored, deseeded
  and diced
2 tablespoons pitted and halved
  black olives
I tablespoon chopped fresh thyme
salt and freshly ground black pepper
100ml tomato juice

CAPER AÏOLI
2 cloves roasted garlic, chopped
1 egg yolk
1 teaspoon mustard
1 teaspoon lemon juice
100ml olive oil
1 teaspoon capers
salt and freshly ground black pepper

KINGFISH STEAKS
4 x 180g kingfish steaks
salt and freshly ground black pepper
olive oil

Heat the olive oil in a hot frying pan and toss in the beans, onion, capsicum, olives and thyme. Season with salt and pepper and sauté for 4 minutes. Add the tomato juice and reduce slightly until tomato juice thickens and coats the vegetables.

For the aïoli, put the garlic, egg yolk, mustard and lemon juice in a bowl. Whisk together and slowly drizzle in the olive oil drop by drop while you whisk to form an emulsion. Add a little warm water if it is too thick; it should be the consistency of half-whipped cream. Stir in the capers and season with salt and pepper.

Season both sides of the kingfish steaks with salt and pepper, then drizzle with olive oil. Fry on a hot grill plate or in a grill pan for 3 minutes on each side.

Place a small amount of the warm salad on each of 4 serving plates, top with a kingfish steak and drizzle with the caper aïoli.

To get the best grill pattern on the fish for a smart presentation, make sure the grill plate is hot and the fish is lightly smeared with olive oil.

HOROPITO HAPUKU FILLETS, SWEET CHILLI PEPPER JAM ON CHERRY TOMATO & PARENGO SALAD Serves 4

HAPUKU FILLETS
4 x 200g hapuku fillets
1 tablespoon horopito pepper
salt
3 tablespoons butter
50ml olive oil

SWEET CHILLI PEPPER JAM
4 tablespoons vegetable oil
200g shallots, finely diced
1 clove garlic, finely diced
1 red chilli, deseeded and
  finely diced
1 red capsicum, cored, deseeded
  and finely diced
100g brown sugar
2 tablespoons lime juice

CHERRY TOMATO AND PARENGO SALAD
1 punnet cherry tomatoes, halved
½ cup sliced parengo
200ml olive oil
100ml white wine vinegar
1 tablespoon mild mustard
1 teaspoon crushed garlic
1 teaspoon sugar
salt and freshly ground black pepper

For the hapuku fillets, season with horopito pepper and salt. Heat the butter and a little olive in a frying pan, then place the fillets in the pan with the white side down first. Sear for 2 minutes, then turn over to finish cooking. Set aside and keep warm.

For the chilli jam, heat the vegetable oil in a saucepan, then add the shallots, garlic, chilli and capsicum. Sauté lightly for 5 minutes. Add the brown sugar and lime juice and mash the ingredients or process in a blender.

For the salad, arrange the tomatoes on 4 serving plates and garnish with the parengo. In a bowl, whisk together the remaining ingredients and drizzle this dressing over the tomatoes and parengo.

Place a hapuku fillet on each of the 4 plates and top with a tablespoonful of sweet chilli jam. Serve immediately.

PAN-FRIED MAOMAO FILLETS WITH PAWPAW & BANANA SALAD

Serves 6

6 x 120g maomao fillets
salt and freshly ground black pepper
olive oil for frying
50ml lime cordial
100ml cream
¼ cup chopped fresh coriander
1 red chilli, deseeded and chopped
1 teaspoon fish sauce
4 tablespoons sugar
2 bananas, chopped
6 cos lettuce leaves
2 red onions, finely sliced
1 cucumber, peeled and sliced
1 red capsicum, cored, deseeded
  and sliced
1 green capsicum, cored, deseeded
  and sliced
1 pawpaw or rockmelon, peeled and
  sliced

Lightly season the maomao fillets with salt and pepper and pan-fry both sides in a little olive oil until golden and cooked. Remove from the pan and keep warm.

Add the lime cordial, cream, coriander, chilli, fish sauce and sugar to the pan. Season with salt and pepper and bring to the boil. Simmer to reduce. Add the bananas to the sauce, then place the fish in the sauce to warm through.

Place a leaf of cos on each of 6 serving plates and top with some onion, cucumber, capsicum and pawpaw. Place a maomao fillet on each serving and pour the sauce over.

POACHED SALMON STEAKS WITH SAUTÉED CRAYFISH Serves 4

COURT BOUILLON
1 litre water or crayfish stock
300ml white wine
juice of ½ lemon
1 large onion, finely sliced
2 stalks celery
1 bouquet garni
pinch of salt

SALMON AND CRAYFISH
4 x 230g salmon steaks
1 cooked 400g crayfish tail
50g butter
50g flour
1 egg yolk
2 tablespoons cream
salt and freshly ground black pepper
lemon wedges and Italian parsley
  for garnishing

For the court bouillon, place all the ingredients in a large saucepan and bring to the boil. Simmer, uncovered, for 20 minutes. Set aside.

Place the salmon steaks in the bouillon, bring slowly to simmering point then cover and poach for 10 minutes or until the salmon is just cooked. Remove and keep warm. Strain the bouillon, reserving the liquid.

Meanwhile, slice the crayfish tail into 4 medallions. Heat the butter in a frying pan and lightly sauté the crayfish. Remove crayfish from the pan and keep warm.

Stir the flour into the butter and add the strained court bouillon slowly, stirring all the time, until it reaches a sauce-like consistency. Beat the egg yolk and cream together and whisk into the pan. Season with salt and pepper.

To serve, top each salmon steak with a piece of crayfish then drizzle the sauce over. Garnish with lemon wedges and parsley.

CURRIED SNAPPER HEADS Serves 6

1 tablespoon butter
1 large onion, finely chopped
1 teaspoon curry powder
6 snapper heads
500ml water
2 large potatoes, peeled and diced
1 large carrot, peeled and diced
1 teaspoon salt

In a large saucepan melt the butter, then lightly fry the onion until soft. Stir in the curry powder and fry for a further 5 minutes.

Add the fish heads standing them upright then add the water, potato and carrot. Add the salt, cover and steam the fish heads until just cooked (about 10 minutes).

Serve the heads in bowls surrounded by the vegetables.

POACHED SALMON STEAKS WITH SAUTÉED CRAYFISH

THAI BABY SQUID SALAD Serves 4

MARINADE
100ml olive oil
1 teaspoon minced chilli
2 cloves garlic, crushed
50ml soy sauce
50ml sesame oil
1 teaspoon ground coriander
1 teaspoon ground cumin
1 teaspoon Thai seasoning

SQUID SALAD
1kg baby squid tubes
olive oil for frying
50ml rice wine vinegar
grated zest of 2 lemons
200g mesclun salad mix
1 parsnip, peeled and cut into
 thin matchsticks
1 carrot, peeled and cut into
 thin matchsticks

For the marinade, place all the ingredients in a bowl and whisk until well combined.

Slice the squid tubes along one side to reveal the inner flesh. Using a small sharp knife remove any membrane, then score the flesh diagonally in a criss-cross pattern. (Do not cut right through the flesh.) Place the squid in the marinade, cover and refrigerate for at least 2 hours or overnight for the best result.

Heat some olive oil in a wok or frying pan. Add the marinated squid to the wok. Fry for 30 seconds, then remove from pan. Add the rice wine vinegar and lemon zest and return the squid to the pan and quickly warm through.

Place the mesclun salad mix, carrot and parsnip in a bowl. Arrange the squid around the salad and use the juices as the dressing. Serve straight away.

To get the squid tube to curl properly, the pan has to be hot and the criss-cross pattern needs to be cut on the inside of the tube.

Although I obviously enjoy cooking meat and seafood, you may be surprised to learn that I spent my early years as a trainee chef mastering the art of desserts. During my apprenticeship I was given the opportunity to create five special desserts for the restaurant trolley every night: a cheesecake, a mousse, fruit salad, a gâteau and a flan.

I know there are chefs out there who prefer to skip desserts and head straight to the front line. Yes, it's a fiddly job that requires flair and patience, but once you master the art of dessert-making, you'll find it's a piece of cake! I'm glad I was given the opportunity to start on desserts. Flour, sugar, baking powder and vanilla essence are great staples to keep in your pantry. Pancakes for breakfast, anyone? Or how about a freshly baked banana cake?

I remember the days I cheated in home economics class during my intermediate school days. I used to double my cake and biscuit recipes to achieve a larger yield. It didn't take long for the teacher to catch on, but it was good while it lasted. Heaps of cookies for my mates!

Once you have mastered the sweet desserts in this section, I recommend you try your hand at the rewena bread and the kumara and horopito bread – there's nothing like freshly baked, home-made bread with a little bit of butter, jam and a nice cup of tea. Give these recipes a go – they're simple but very, very tasty.

Mauri Kai, Mauri Ora!

SWEETS & BREADS

HE PURINI, HE PARAOA

STEAMED CHOCOLATE PUDDINGS WITH CHOCOLATE SAUCE Serves 3

STEAMED PUDDINGS

110g butter

110g caster sugar

2 eggs

85g plain flour

1 teaspoon baking powder

3 tablespoons cocoa powder

30g ground almonds

CHOCOLATE SAUCE

100ml cream

100g dark chocolate

50ml honey liqueur or wine

4 strawberries to serve

1 cup blueberries to serve

whipped cream to serve

icing sugar for dusting

For the steamed puddings, cream the butter and sugar in a bowl, then whisk in the eggs. In a separate bowl sieve the flour, baking powder and cocoa and stir in the ground almonds. Gradually fold into the egg mixture.

Grease 3 dariole moulds with butter. (You can use coffee cups if you don't have moulds.) Fill each mould with pudding mixture, then place in a wide saucepan. Pour boiling water into the pan until it is three-quarters of the way up the sides of the moulds. Place over a medium heat, cover and steam the puddings for 30-35 minutes. Check the water level occasionally to make sure it doesn't evaporate. The puddings are ready when a knife inserted in the centre comes out clean. If there is some mixture stuck to the knife, steam them for a further 5 minutes.

For the chocolate sauce, place all the ingredients in a saucepan over a medium heat and leave for 10 minutes. The mixture will melt and start to reduce. Set aside and keep warm.

To serve, place the unmoulded puddings on plates with a drizzle of chocolate sauce. Garnish with strawberries, blueberries and fresh cream, and dust with icing sugar.

BOMBE ALASKA Serves 2

5 egg whites
1 cup caster sugar
1 x 30 x 20 cm trifle sponge
2 nips banana liqueur
4 scoops vanilla ice-cream
2 tablespoons chopped peaches
2 tablespoons raspberries, fresh or
 defrosted from frozen

Preheat the oven to 180°C. Beat the egg whites until white and fluffy, then add the sugar a little at a time, whisking until the egg whites form stiff peaks.

Cut 2 circles out of the sponge and place each on an ovenproof serving plate. Drizzle a little banana liqueur or brandy onto the sponge and arrange 2 scoops of ice cream on top of the sponge.

Using a piping bag or spatula, cover the sides of the ice-cream and sponge with the egg-white meringue. Before covering the top, spoon on the peaches and raspberries and finish with the meringue.

Bake in the oven for 3 minutes or until golden. Carefully remove the bombes from the oven and, just before serving, heat a capful of the banana liqueur or some brandy in a ladle over an open flame. When it starts to flame, pour it over the desserts. Serve immediately.

Some steps of this dessert can be prepared in advance. Roll the ice-cream and place on the sponge, then store in the freezer until required.

BERRY & BANANA PANCAKE STACK
Serves 2

1 cup self-raising flour
1½ tablespoons caster sugar
½ teaspoon salt
1 egg, lightly beaten
¾ cup milk
60g butter, melted, plus extra
  for frying
1 cup seasonal berries
½ cup icing sugar
1 banana, sliced
whipped cream to serve
maple syrup to serve
strawberries for garnishing

Place the flour, sugar and salt in a food processor or blender. In a separate bowl, combine the egg, milk and butter. Pour the liquid mixture into the food processor or blender while the machine is still running and mix until smooth.

Place spoonfuls of the mixture in a hot, greased frying pan over a medium heat. Cook until bubbles form on the surface, then turn over and cook the other side until golden brown.

Heat the berries in a saucepan with half the icing sugar and a little water. Simmer for 5 minutes. Serve the pancakes warm with some berry compote, sliced banana, whipped cream, maple syrup and strawberries. Dust each serving with remaining icing sugar.

Everybody loves banana pancakes for breakfast. Try using fresh slices of rockmelon or mango instead of banana and berries for a more refreshing version.

BLACKBERRY & APPLE CRUMBLE
Serves 6

1kg apples, peeled, cored and diced
150g fresh blackberries
½ cup raisins
¼ cup caster sugar
2 teaspoons cinnamon
100g butter, melted
100g sugar
1 cup rolled oats
1 cup muesli
ice-cream and sliced apple to serve
fresh mint leaves for garnishing

Preheat the oven to 180°C.

In a saucepan, combine the apples, blackberries, raisins, caster sugar and 1 teaspoon cinnamon. Heat on a low-medium heat until the sugar dissolves and everything is well combined. Pour into a baking dish.

To prepare the crumble, mix together the melted butter and sugar. Mix in the rolled oats, muesli and remaining cinnamon. Spoon the crumble over the apple and blackberry mixture and bake for 20 minutes.

Serve with ice-cream, sliced apple and fresh mint.

BLUEBERRY BREAD PUDDING Serves 4

1 x day-old baguette
3 large eggs, beaten
2¼ cups milk
3 tablespoons sugar
1 teaspoon vanilla extract
1 cup blueberries
½ cup plain flour
¼ cup dark brown sugar
½ teaspoon ground cinnamon
100g butter, diced
1 cup strawberries

Cut the bread into 10 diagonal slices. Arrange in a greased baking dish.

Whisk together the eggs, milk, sugar and vanilla. Pour the egg mixture over the bread slices, cover and refrigerate for 1 hour.

Preheat the oven to 180°C. Sprinkle the blueberries over the bread mixture. Place the flour, brown sugar and cinnamon in a blender, add the butter and mix until crumbly. Sprinkle the mixture over the blueberries.

Bake, uncovered, for 40-45 minutes or until set and golden. Serve immediately with strawberries.

You can use either fresh or frozen berry fruit for this delicious dessert. If using frozen, thaw prior to using.

HONEY APPLE TURNOVERS
Serves 4

1 tablespoon raisins
3 tablespoons finely chopped walnuts
½ teaspoon ground cinnamon,
  plus extra for dusting
6 tablespoons honey
2 large baking apples
250g shortcrust pastry

Preheat the oven to 180°C. In a small bowl, combine the raisins, walnuts and cinnamon, then stir in half the honey.

Peel the apples and cut each in half lengthways. Trim away the stems and scoop out the core from each half with a melon baller, making a wide hole for the filling. Divide the honey mixture evenly among the apple centres.

Form the pastry into 4 balls. Flatten each into a 15cm round, about 5mm thick. Place a round of dough over each apple half with filling side up, then wrap the dough around each apple. Trim to fit and pinch the edges underneath the apples to seal entirely.

Combine 1 tablespoon of honey with 1 teaspoon of hot water. Stir until the honey dissolves. Brush the mixture over the top of each apple and dust with the extra cinnamon. Transfer the turnovers to a baking tray lined with baking paper and bake for about 35 minutes until the turnovers are golden. Remove from oven and drizzle with the remaining honey. Serve warm or at room temperature.

SWEET & SPICY PUMPKIN PIE
Serves 6

PASTRY
1½ cups plain flour
¼ cup icing sugar
100g cold butter, diced
1 egg yolk
1–2 tablespoons iced water

FILLING
500g crown pumpkin, peeled,
  deseeded and cut into chunks
¾ cup golden syrup
4 eggs, lightly beaten
½ cup cream
1 teaspoon cinnamon
¼ teaspoon ground nutmeg
whipped cream to serve

For the pastry, sift the flour and icing sugar into a bowl. Rub the butter into the flour until the mixture resembles coarse breadcrumbs. Add the yolk and just enough water to mix to a stiff dough. (This can be done in a food processor.) Roll the dough into a ball, cover with plastic food wrap and refrigerate for 30 minutes.

For the filling, boil the pumpkin in salted water until tender. Drain well, mix in the golden syrup while still hot, then mix in the other ingredients until well combined.

Preheat the oven to 190°C. Roll out the pastry on a lightly floured surface to fit a 24cm flan dish. Line the dish with the pastry and trim off any excess. Prick the base and refrigerate for 10 minutes, then bake blind for 10 minutes. Remove the beans and bake for another 4 minutes to dry out the base.

Pour the filling into the pastry case and bake for 45 minutes at 180°C or until the filling has set. Serve warm with whipped cream.

Give this recipe a try and once you have mastered it, use kumara mash instead of the pumpkin. You will end up with a yellow-coloured sweet and spicy kumara pie. Alternatively, try a blend of orange and purple kumara.

PEAR PANCAKE PIE Serves 6

¼ cup sugar

⅓ teaspoon ground cinnamon

3 large eggs

½ cup milk

zest of 1 lemon

½ cup plain flour

½ cup unsalted butter, cut into
  2cm cubes

2 pears, peeled, cored and cut into
  5mm slices

Preheat the oven to 180°C. In a small bowl, mix the sugar with the cinnamon and set aside.

In a medium-sized bowl, lightly whisk the eggs, milk and lemon zest. Mix in the flour until just combined.

In a 25cm ovenproof skillet, melt half the butter over a medium heat. Add the pears and sauté for 5 minutes or until tender. Pour the batter over the pears and transfer the skillet to the oven. Bake for 20 minutes or until the pears are tender and the pie rises.

Meanwhile, melt the remaining butter. Remove the skillet from the oven, drizzle the pie with the butter and sprinkle with the cinnamon and sugar mixture.

Return the pie to the oven for 5 minutes or until the sugar mixture is bubbling. Serve immediately.

Firm pears are better to use in this recipe. They are easier to handle and, once cooked, will still keep their shape for a better presentation.

RHUBARB & APPLE SPONGE
Serves 6

2kg rhubarb, chopped into 2cm strips
2 medium apples, peeled, cored and
  thinly sliced lengthways
⅓ cup sugar
1 teaspoon grated lemon zest
¼ cup water
2 eggs
3 tablespoons cornflour
3 tablespoons plain flour
3 tablespoons self-raising flour
fresh fruit and ice-cream to serve

Preheat the oven to 180°C. Place the rhubarb, apples, half the sugar, lemon zest and water in a large saucepan over a high heat and bring to the boil. Reduce the heat, cover the pan and simmer for 15 minutes or until the fruit is tender. Pour the hot rhubarb mixture into a deep, greased ovenproof dish.

Place the eggs in a bowl and beat with an electric mixer until thick and creamy. Gradually add the remaining sugar, beating after each addition until dissolved. Sift the flours over the egg mixture and gently fold through. Spread the mixture evenly over the hot rhubarb mixture and bake for 30 minutes.

Serve with fresh fruit and ice-cream.

When buying rhubarb, choose fresh, young, dark-pink stalks, which are sweeter and a lot more tender. Stand the stalks in cold water for an hour or so to refresh them.

WHITE CHOCOLATE BAVAROIS
WITH TAMARILLOS Serves 6

2 egg yolks
100g sugar
500ml milk
200ml cream
40g white chocolate buttons
12g (2 tablespoons) gelatine

TAMARILLOS
4 tamarillos
2 tablespoons sugar

Whisk the egg yolks with half the sugar. Heat the milk and 100ml of the cream with the remaining sugar. Stir in the white chocolate buttons until melted.

Dissolve the gelatine in a little water over heat. Add to the egg and sugar mixture. Stir the milk into the egg mixture. Place the bowl over a basin with ice-cold water and whisk until thick. Half-whip the remaining cream and fold into the mixture.

Pour into bavarois moulds or cups and refrigerate overnight.

For the tamarillos, cut the fruit in half, scoop out the flesh and heat in a saucepan with the sugar and a little water. Blend when the flesh is soft. Pour over the unmoulded white chocolate bavarois to serve.

REWENA BREAD

Makes 1 loaf

3 tablespoons sugar
1½ tablespoon yeast granules
1 litre warm water
1.5kg plain flour
butter for greasing baking dish

Mix the sugar and yeast with the water.

Place the flour in a large bowl, make a well in the centre and add the yeast and sugar mixture. Mix the ingredients until they bind together.

Turn out the dough on a lightly floured surface and knead until smooth, then roll into desired shape.

Place the dough in a greased baking dish and place the baking dish next to a warmer drawer or warm oven for 30–45 minutes to allow the dough to rise.

Bake in the oven at 200°C for 10 minutes, then reduce the temperature to 180°C and bake for a further 50 minutes.

When cooked remove from the oven and place a damp tea towel on top to keep the bread moist.

PUMPKIN & FLAXSEED BREAD
Makes 1 loaf

1 pumpkin, halved and deseeded
1½ cups plain flour
½ teaspoon salt
1 cup sugar
1 teaspoon baking soda
½ cup flaxseed oil
1 tablespoon flax seeds
2 eggs, beaten
¼ cup water
½ teaspoon ground nutmeg
½ teaspoon ground cinnamon
½ teaspoon ground allspice
½ cup chopped walnuts

Place the pumpkin halves face down on an oven tray lined with baking paper or aluminium foil. Bake at 180°C until soft (about 45 minutes to 1 hour). Cool, then scoop out the flesh and mash. Or, if you are working with pumpkin pieces, roast or boil them until tender, then remove and discard the skin. Set aside 1 cup of the mash and freeze the remainder for future use.

Preheat the oven to 180°C. Sift together the flour, salt, sugar and baking soda.

Mix together the reserved pumpkin mash, oil, flax seeds, eggs, water and spices, then combine with the dry ingredients, but do not mix too thoroughly. Stir in the walnuts.

Pour into a well-buttered 23cm x 13cm x 7cm loaf pan. Bake for 50-60 minutes until a thin skewer poked in the very centre of the loaf comes out clean. Turn out of the pan and leave to cool on a rack. Serve alongside Bacon Hock and Watercress Soup (see page 12) or spread with home-made plum jam or manuka honey.

CARROT & KUMARA CAKE Serves 6

6 eggs
1 cup canola oil
4 cups plain flour
2 cups sugar
6 teaspoons baking soda
1 teaspoon ground cinnamon
5 cups grated carrot
1 cup grated kumara
1 cup chopped walnuts
2 teaspoons grated orange zest

ICING
2 tablespoons softened butter
¼ cup traditional cream cheese
1 cup icing sugar
1 teaspoon grated lemon zest
juice of ½ lemon

For the cake, preheat the oven to 180°C. Beat the eggs in a bowl, then stir in the oil.

Sift the flour, sugar, baking soda and cinnamon into the egg and oil mixture, and mix to combine.

Add the carrot, kumara, walnuts and orange zest, mixing well. Pour into a greased 20cm cake tin and bake for 40 minutes. Remove from the oven and cool on a wire rack.

For the icing, beat the butter and cream cheese until creamy. Mix in the icing sugar, lemon zest and juice, and beat until well combined.

Ice the cooled cake and serve immediately or store in cool place until required.

KUMARA & HOROPITO BREAD
Makes 1 loaf

1 cup milk

2 tablespoons butter

1 tablespoon sugar

1 teaspoon salt

7g (2½ teaspoons) dry yeast

¼ cup warm water

1 tablespoon snipped chives

1 tablespoon horopito pepper

1kg plain flour

2 cups mashed or puréed kumara

Heat the milk, butter, sugar and salt in a saucepan over low heat until the butter melts. Remove from the heat and allow to cool.

Combine the yeast with the warm water, stirring until dissolved, then stir into the milk mixture. Place in a large mixing bowl.

Fold the chives, horopito and 1 cup of flour into the mashed kumara and add to the mixing bowl. Beat together until smooth. Keep adding the remaining flour until a stiff dough forms. Place the dough on a floured surface and knead until smooth and elastic. Add more flour if the dough is too moist.

Place the dough in a large oiled bowl and cover with a clean tea towel. Set aside near a warm stove and allow the dough to prove for about 1 hour.

Punch the dough down and place on a floured surface. Shape into a loaf and place in a greased 23cm x 13cm x 7cm loaf tin. Cover with the tea towel and allow to prove again for another 40 minutes.

Preheat the oven to 190°C. Bake the bread for 35-45 minutes. Serve with chicken liver pâté or smoked eel.

If you can't get hold of horopito pepper, substitute fresh or dried herbs to your liking. I use freshly chopped thyme, which blends well with kumara.

MAORI GLOSSARY

hangi	Traditional Maori underground oven
heki	egg
hinaki	eel trap
hinamona	cinnamon
hinu hua whenua	vegetable oil
hinu oriwa	olive oil
hua maroke pango	blackcurrants
hua maroke whero	redcurrants
huka	sugar
inanga	whitebait
kai	food
kai moana	seafood
kakahi	freshwater mussels
kamokamo	courgette
kapeti	cabbage
karakia	prayer
kewai	freshwater crayfish
kina	sea urchin
kirimi kakati	sour cream
koro	grandfather
koura	freshwater and saltwater crayfish
kumara penupenu	mashed kumara
miere	honey
miiti kaawhe	veal loin or fillet
miraka	milk
parani	brandy
paraoa parai	fried bread
pata	butter
peihana	pheasant
pepa pango	black pepper
pikopiko	fern shoot
poaka tauraki	ham
puehu paprika	ground paprika
puehu paraoa	flour
riiki	onion
riiki roa	leek
riwai penupenu	mashed potato
rohimere	rosemary
Tane Mahuta	God of the forest
Tangaroa	God of the sea
tiamu hua maroke pango	blackcurrant jam
tiamu karepe tauraki	redcurrant jam
tihi	cheese
toroi	fermented food
tote	salt
wai remana me tona kiri	lemon juice and zest
waina poota	port
waina reka	sherry
wairenga	gravy or broth
waka	canoe
whanau	family

CULINARY GLOSSARY

aïoli strongly flavoured garlic mayonnaise typical of the Provençe region in France.

al dente Italian phrase meaning 'to the tooth', referring to the desired end result of cooked pasta. It should offer a slight resistance to the bite.

bake blind to bake a pastry shell before it is filled, usually because the filling will need less cooking time than the pastry. The pastry is usually pricked with a fork, then lined with baking paper or aluminium foil and covered with dried beans or rice until cooked.

bavarois French term for Bavarian cream, a cold dessert of custard, cream, flavourings and gelatine.

beurre blanc meaning 'white butter' is a classic French sauce of reduced wine, vinegar and shallots into which cold butter is whisked.

bisque a rich seafood purée, often including wine, cognac and cream, used as the basis of a soup that has seafood added.

bouquet garni a selection of herbs, usually parsley, thyme and a bay leaf, wrapped in muslin, tied and used to flavour soups, stocks and sauces and removed before serving.

Caprese a salad of fresh mozzarella, tomato and basil leaves, drizzled with olive oil.

ceviche a dish of raw fish 'cooked' in citrus juice.

compote fresh or dried fruit cooked slowly in sugar for a dessert or dessert accompaniment.

court bouillon aromatic stock or broth used for poaching fish and seafood.

dariole mould a small, cylindrical mould mostly used for desserts.

deglaze to pour hot stock or wine into a pan in which meat has been cooked to loosen up the caramelised juices, thus enriching sauces and gravies.

egg wash beaten egg, usually with water, brushed over food to be baked, such as pastry and bread.

glaze in savoury dishes, a reduced meat stock.

flax seeds produced from the flax plant, these seeds are most commonly pressed to make oil but are also lovely sprinkled over breads and pastries.

horopito pepper a variety of pepper that comes from the native horopito tree which is very hot and leaves a burning aftertaste. Available from good delicatessens and gourmet food stores.

jus 'juice' in French, though in cookery it usually refers to gravy made with the pan juices from roast meat mixed with stock or wine simmered until reduced and thickened a little.

kawakawa pepper a variety of pepper that comes from the native kawakawa tree. Available from good delicatessens and gourmet food stores.

medallion small, round piece of meat.

mornay a béchamel sauce flavoured with cheese, sometimes stock and wine, which may be enriched with cream and eggs.

mozzarella soft, milky white Italian cheese traditionally made with buffalo milk and eaten fresh.

Provençale dishes cooked with typical ingredients of the Provence region of France, including olive oil, garlic, tomatoes, anchovies and olives.

rice wine vinegar widely used in Japanese cooking. Also used in marinades and glazes.

rösti a potato cake made from thin slices or grated potato and fried until crisp and golden.

roulade food, usually meat, rolled around a filling and secured.

surimi pulped fish formed into shapes like crab sticks.

velouté a white sauce made with stock instead of milk, often used as the basis of soups.

vol-au-vent a round case of puff pastry, filled for an entrée or hors d'oeuvre.

WEIGHTS & MEASURES

The following amounts have been rounded up or down for convenience.

Abbreviations

g	gram
kg	kilogram
mm	millimetre
cm	centimetre
ml	millilitre
°C	degrees Celsius

Weight conversions

10-15 g	½ ounce
20g	¾ ounce
25g	1 ounces
40g	1½ ounces
50g	2 ounces
75g	3 ounces
100g	3½ ounces
125g	4½ ounces
150g	5 ounces
175g	6 ounces
200g	7 ounces
225g	8 ounces
250g	9 ounces
275g	9½ ounces
300g	10½ ounces
350g	12½ ounces
400g	14 ounces
450g	16 ounces (1 lb)
500g	17½ ounces
600g	21 ounces
750g	26½ ounces
1kg	35 ounces

Baking tin sizes

15cm	6 inches
18cm	7 inches
20cm	8 inches
23cm	9 inches
25cm	10 inches
28cm	11 inches

Liquid conversions

50ml	1¾ fluid ounces
75ml	2½ fluid ounces
100ml	3½ fluid ounces
125ml	4 fluid ounces
150ml	5 fluid ounces
175ml	6 fluid ounces
200ml	7 fluid ounces
225ml	8 fluid ounces
250ml	8½ fluid ounces
300ml	10 fluid ounces
400ml	13½ fluid ounces
500ml	17 fluid ounces
600ml	20 fluid ounces
750ml	25 fluid ounces
1 litre	34 fluid ounces

A pint in the UK is 16 fluid ounces
A pint in the USA is 20 fluid ounces

Spoon measures

¼ teaspoon	1.25ml
½ teaspoon	2.5ml
1 teaspoon	5ml
1 tablespoon	15ml

NB: The Australian tablespoon is 20ml

Oven temperatures

Celsius	Fahrenheit	Gas Mark
100°C	225°F	¼
125°C	250°F	½
150°C	300°F	2
160°C	320°F	3
170°C	340°F	3
180°C	350°F	4
190°C	375°F	5
200°C	400°F	6
210°C	410°F	7
220°C	425°F	7
230°C	450°F	8
250°C	500°F	9

INDEX

Italicised numbers indicate recipe photographs